Never in

Octavia –

With best wishes,

Julian

H.G

Never in a Fishbowl

(A Minnow in the Sea of Life)

JULIA HARLEY-GREEN

© Julia Harley-Green, 2022

Published by Cory Publishing

A CIP catalogue record for this book is available from the British Library.

ISBN 978-1-7390807-0-9

Book layout and cover design by Clare Brayshaw

Front cover Illustration 66124595 © Sergei Mokhov | Dreamstime.com

Prepared and printed by:

York Publishing Services Ltd
64 Hallfield Road
Layerthorpe
York YO31 7ZQ

Tel: 01904 431213

Website: www.yps-publishing.co.uk

For my nieces and nephews
And my stepson, Zareh

Acknowledgements

Incorporated in this work are excerpts from articles I wrote for *The Sydney Morning Herald; The Bulletin; The Palm Beach Daily News;* and *Ocean Drive's Palm Beach Magazine.*

My thanks to those who read through early drafts, in particular Susannah Kurti and Nicola Lisle. Also to Carolyn Wilson who proffered advice and encouragement as we walked through our local park, and to Rosanella Di Costanzo who calmed me when I grew exasperated with my computer.

Contents

Introduction ix

1 Setting Sail 1

2 Coming to America 13

3 Food Follies 26

4 Eleven Seconds 39

5 Life as a Global Volunteer 53

6 At Home... 69

7 Luca 82

8 Palm Beach 96

9 Men 113

10 Life's a Production 126

Introduction

I was born in Hertfordshire during the dismal winter of 1947. The Second World War caused a lull in my parents' burgeoning family of two small girls while my father was away in the Royal Air Force fighting over Burma (now Myanmar). Never mind, on his return, the family increased with twin girls of whom I was one. My mother would have tried for more, in the hope of diversity and a son, but my father determined enough was enough.

The following is a record of events in my life, those that have left a sombre and indelible mark, and those that make me smile or laugh out loud. It is not in chronological order. I have omitted episodes that I consider meaningless, flagrantly diabolic (you might not agree) or just plain ordinary. I was a late starter, reluctant to study. In my mid-teens I regarded my life as divided between two prisons, that of boarding school and a country house detached from youthful civilization. Later, after the slow beginning, I became enthused with learning and took numerous courses, a degree, and studied all things cultural. I remain addicted to discovery and for as long as my legs will carry me and my eyes can read, will stalk that road with avid curiosity.

More importantly, I have been fortunate until now to have enjoyed good health. This has enabled me to travel extensively and thereby to meet others, rich and poor, all of whom have contributed enormously to what follows. My views, where there are any, and I've tried on the whole not to impose them, are mine and mine alone.

Setting Sail

Finding my sea-legs – Antingham Lodge –
rations and manners – the travels begin

Early in 2002 I had just boarded ship to sail down the coast of Chile and round Cape Horn when rumour flew among the passengers that the liner had only one stabiliser and we could be in for rough seas. I am not a good sailor so before leaving home and flying to board the ship in Valparaiso, I had consulted my doctor and requested medication in case of inclement weather. The doctor dismissed my pleas with an airy wave of the hand and effectively called me a sissy. "You'll be fine," he assured me. "Ships have stabilisers. You don't need a prescription!" Unconvinced, I went to my local pharmacy and bought a tube of twelve tablets for the prevention of travel sickness.

On board the first evening and having barely unpacked, a calm sea gave way to an increasing swell and spray hit the decks. My worst fears were confirmed when the captain's voice announced over the tannoy that the ship had indeed damaged a stabiliser during the previous voyage. "Probably hit a whale," he announced glibly, before adding words to the effect that there was no need to worry. To say I was disconcerted would be an understatement. I sat in my cabin contemplating my small tube of tablets and how long they might last. If there was a prolonged spell of rough weather, the last thing I wanted was to end up helplessly incapacitated before the ship's doctor. I had heard of horrible actions taken to relieve nausea such as a potent shot that knocked you out for the best part of 24 hours or, even worse, the use of suppositories.

Next morning there was a trickle of passengers at the breakfast buffet. The ship was rockin' and rollin' and the exterior decks were flooding. Surprisingly, I felt fine so I picked gingerly at a bread roll and eggs then retreated back to my cabin. As a precautionary measure, I opened my tube of tablets, removed one, carefully dissected it and swallowed one half. Feeling dejected, I lay on my bed and miserably contemplated the end of the world. After an hour or so, I chastised myself for being ridiculous, rose from my deathbed and took the remaining half pill. To my surprise, come lunchtime I was raring to eat again and scampered up a few decks to an uncrowded restaurant. There I ate a loaded plate before taking a stroll round the ship. By this time the swell had begun to subside and by dinner time most of the passengers emerged and the cruise began in earnest. For the next three weeks, including sailing around Cape Horn where weather conditions have been known to deteriorate, it was as if the ship was floating on a duck pond. When I flew home from Rio de Janeiro, I still had eleven pills.

I will never be a great sailor but my life's course has been akin to a cruise, a few days of rough sailing here and there but mostly calm seas. In retrospect, rough times tend to fade while happy periods mushroom into gleeful memories. On many occasions, including the start of that South American trip, I feared the worst and it never happened.

At age five, I knew nothing of the vagaries of high seas; life centred around personal pleasure, not least food. My only fear was of the dark but, as I shared a bedroom with my twin sister, Mary, I was rarely alone after dusk. Our family holidays were always a highlight, and these now form some of my fondest memories. Every summer we stayed in our Norfolk home, a converted watermill near North Walsham, about 120 miles from London. This magical place provided days of discovery and excitement and were among the happiest of my childhood.

Antingham Lodge stood in front of a lake stretching back as far as the eye could see, ending in a vague yellow-green haze of reeds and bulrushes. Of the mill, only the large waterwheel remained, the lower spokes resting in a few inches of water and covered in long strands of slimy weed. As the water trickled out of the lake, it passed beneath the wheel and down a tiny waterfall into the paddock beyond. The upper spokes, well clear of the water, were covered in moss.

The lodge faced sideways to the drive and a tall wooden arch separated the lawn from the gravel. The walls were covered in creeper, long green tendrils of giant ivy climbing over the wooden supports to the roof. Inside, the rooms ran into one another; there were no dividing passageways, no hall or porch. The only way to walk the length of the building without passing through any of the rooms was along the balcony where, at the end by the waterwheel, a set of steep wooden steps led down to the ground. Many of the rooms had a strange musty smell due to the proximity of the water and the rough timber beams which were an integral part of the structure.

Being young, exploring was a feature of each day, right up there with mealtimes. I knew how to swim so the lake held no qualms and plenty of treasure, not all of it clean or clear but invariably compelling with its mysteries and wonder. At the far end of the lake, the water grew shallow and the mud was soft and thick. Wild duck swam between the reeds, kingfishers waited patiently on the branches of the willow trees and herons picked their way cautiously through the marsh. In late spring, the duck paraded their young, watching anxiously in case the chicks were snapped up by marauding young pike or carried off by hawks. Each year, the two resident swans built their nest on a tiny island of woven reeds and mud. While one of the birds sat on the nest, the other made occasional forays into the nearby rushes for food. Now and then, the one in the water would sit preening, its long neck arching over backwards as it ruffled its plumage or snuffled into the thick layers of down. For some time before the young chicks hatched, the swans swam singly to the landing stage by the lodge. Whether it was the same bird each time, or whether they took it in turns, we never knew. Finally, when the cygnets were old enough to look after themselves, they were chased away by their parents to find territories of their own.

From my bedroom window overlooking the drive, I could see the edge of the paddock with the stream running through it and the road close by. The road passed over a narrow humpback bridge and down the other side to an inn. Cattle grazed in the field and near the bridge shone the bright gold petals of thousands of marsh marigolds. Along the road, pressed into the surface, were numerous small dark shadows which had once been toads. Some had been dead for months but here and there a new corpse, not yet squashed flat by passing motorists, stared up angrily, its shape distorted, its eyes disgorged in a horrid parody of death. This roadkill stayed in my mind, an awesome introduction into life's cycle and the toll taken by the toads and their vulnerable struggle to cross the road.

Never a day passed without there being something different to do. When the weather was warm, we jumped into the water from the landing stage and swam round to the boathouse. There, nesting beneath the thatched eaves, swallows swooped in and out, their beaks crammed full of dried grass, or food if their young had already hatched.

In the boathouse, a rowing boat shared the mooring space with a small sailing dinghy. We used the rowing boat when we went fishing for pike that rested beneath the shadows of the overhanging trees at the edge of the lake. One summer, the dinghy was towed behind the rowing boat out of the boathouse and round to the landing stage. When we unravelled the sails on the grass in front of the lodge, we discovered a pair of mice had made their home in the rolled-up cloth during the previous winter. Not only had they chewed it into an unrecognisable bundle of rags, but they had rapidly reproduced. By the time we found them, there were at least thirty, the smallest only a few days old.

Early one morning during our last holiday at Antingham Lodge, a flock of strange swans arrived on the lake. Until then, our two resident birds had always managed to head off would-be intruders, but this time there were too many of the alien birds and our own pair stayed at the far end by their nest. The flock circled the lake several times before landing, their wings flapping noisily as they passed overhead. When eventually they decided to settle, descending en masse, their great webbed feet stretched out beneath them as, half running and half slipping, they lowered their giant bodies into the water. They swam to the landing stage in a great mob, pirouetting around and hissing loudly at one another. For a few days, it seemed they intended to stay. Sometimes they left the water and paraded along the mud and shingle at the edge or on the small square patch of lawn in front of the lodge. Then one evening, as unexpectedly as they arrived, they left. As they beat their retreat slowly over the water, there came the reverberating thunder of their wings as slowly and painstakingly they lifted their immense bodies into the air and were gone.

When Antingham Lodge was sold – my two elder sisters were now teenagers and looking for human company over birds and fish – future summer holidays took the form of short hotel stays in various parts of Britain. Swans played no part in my life for nearly sixty years. Today I watch them on several stretches of water in London's Kensington Gardens, close to my flat. I fantasise that the birds I see now could be two or three generations away from those I watched as a child. With a lifespan of up to thirty years in a protected environment, their ancestors might have flown south, trekking from lake to river en route to London. If push came to shove, they could make a meal of short-cropped grass in place of aquatic vegetation, frogs and worms.

I have been fortunate in that my next meal has never been a problem. I do remember years of rationing following the Second World War, particularly the limits per person per week on confectionery. Then my mother placed the week's allowance in a drawer and every Sunday with due ceremony our allotted amounts were brought out and choices were made. This usually meant that my eldest sister chose first and I, being the youngest of four girls by just half an hour, took what was left. But if I remonstrated over life being unfair, years later I witnessed how others managed on far less.

In the early 80s, I toured Ethiopia. While I was sitting at a table waiting for dinner, I first saw what was important when people sit down to eat together. I had spent the morning riding a mule up rugged hillside to see mountain caves, followed by an afternoon peering into ancient underground churches. The meal was set on a long table in a type of hostelry and excited villagers came by to witness the spectacle of a group of foreigners sitting down to eat. Before long a lady approached with a tray of thinly sliced *injera* bread (a wholewheat and slightly spongy flatbread) and slapped a pile down to the left of each guest. Plates of meat and salad had already been set in the centre of the table. According to custom, everyone took a slice of their bread, held it in the palm of one hand and filled it with the choicest morsels from the plates in front of them. Once filled, the bread was rolled up neatly and presented to the head guest or one of our neighbours. We all ate with our fingers and nobody took food for themselves.

Not surprisingly, this tradition ensures you don't nab the best for yourself. I'm not sure what happens to the last piece of food but I'm willing to bet there's no snatch and grab. Since that time I have eaten in some wonderful restaurants and private homes. I have sat at tables with cut glasses, linen napkins, beautiful cutlery, tablecloths and china, yet it is that meal that stays with me for its selfless custom and simplicity.

Also in Ethiopia, water was a precious commodity. Beyond the capital, Addis Ababa, women carried pitchers on their heads and walked miles to and from the nearest well. In one poor urban area, I was given a room that in effect was an exalted hut. Once inside, I walked round testing everything from the faucets to the pull-chain water closet high above the toilet. I was unpacking my bag when there came a knock at the door and my guide stood outside enquiring earnestly if everything was all right. "Take care with the cistern," he warned. "You can flush the toilet only once while you are here." He shrugged sadly: "That's how it is." I drew a quick breath and nodded; I could not bring myself to admit that I had flushed the toilet without need. Since then, in countries where I know there's a water shortage, I check the cistern when I arrive. If there is water, I never flush it. And if the closet is perched overhead then I resist the temptation to pull the chord. I felt remorseful not only because I had wasted a precious commodity but because I should have known better. In my twenties, on a camping trip through north and central Australia, I first experienced daily restrictions due to a restricted water supply. Every visitor arriving in the small opal mining town of Coober Pedy in South Australia was handed a small round pot that held perhaps half a gallon of water. For an overnight stay, this was to cover all ablutions from washing one's face to cleaning teeth and soaping all over. When face and teeth were done, the remaining water was tipped into an overhead inverted bucket with holes in the bottom, and showering followed at breakneck speed.

Other places have the reverse problem; an abundance of non-potable water. More recently I was walking beside rice fields in Vietnam when my guide responded to a man calling out to us from the open front of a house on stilts. When an area is prone to flooding or soggy underfoot, living on stilts is the way to go. In Vietnam such homes are usually made of wood, often with thatched roofing and raised several metres above the ground. The wet season is particularly difficult, and the high homes not only protect against flooding but also keep out vermin.

It seemed we were being invited into the house. The only problem as far as I was concerned was mounting the somewhat insecure ladder. At the best of times I'm not good with heights and with nothing secure to hold onto, my heart starts racing. Gripping the ropes and not looking down, up I went before clambering onto the floor of a sparsely furnished home. Small stools were set out in a semicircle by the open window. Out of the shadows of a dimly lit space emerged at least three generations of a Vietnamese family, all of whom sat down to join us. One of the ladies brought a bottle of clear liquid and some glasses. The man of the house whipped off the cap and began pouring. So it was that at 10.30am I found myself imbibing some potent homemade rice wine and, when I say potent, I mean a liquid akin to Schnapps that seers its way down your throat with biting intent. The owner of the home threw his tot back in a single gulp and watched amused as I played tentatively with mine. The only trouble was, as soon as my glass was half empty, it was promptly replenished. I began wondering whether I'd make it down the ladder when I left.

Children and teenagers emerged from every corner of this ramshackle home, sitting around or in their mothers' laps, watching curiously. I showed them photos of the previous places I had visited in their country and my guide translated. I felt bad at having nothing tangible to offer in return for their hospitality until I remembered that I rarely travel without a few single dollars stuffed in my bag. A paltry offering but they gave the children more pleasure than they were worth.

I doubt many in the family had ever ventured further than the boundaries of local rice fields. Theirs was an overcrowded home devoid of almost everything we take for granted, including fresh running water. To have refused their hospitality would have been out of the question.

Now that I'm older, I have taken to revisiting a few places that meant so much when I first saw them. During the pandemic I took an escorted tour along the Norfolk coast to remember my childhood idyll, viewing the shoreline all the way from Blakeney Harbour to the Norfolk Broads. The scenery was no less enthralling but this time, passing through the glorious countryside in early June, admiring poppies skirting the fields and sniffing gingerly at passing pig farms, I wondered briefly how my life would have been had I lived in a rural area. My second sister, Elizabeth, has made farming her life and has lived in Wales for more than forty years, but I doubt I could have tolerated the human detachment, particularly in winter. For me, living in the centre of a large community has always been paramount.

The small *chariot*, as our touring minibus was euphemistically called, travelled on into Suffolk towards Aldeburgh and the former home of Benjamin Britten and Peter Pears (composer and tenor). And before returning to London, there was one final stop in Dedham Vale, close to the Suffolk-Essex border, an area much loved by the artist, John Constable (1776-1837). As a child, I was bridesmaid at the marriage of Constable's great-great-grandson, Richard, who, as the genes descended, was also destined to paint. Standing at the spot where his ancestor drew inspiration for 'The Hay Wain', now hanging in London's National Gallery, I did feel for a brief moment as if time had paused. Unfortunately, I had no chance to find Antingham Lodge, so who knows if the converted watermill still stands?

Around the time family holidays in Norfolk ended, my family moved from our home near Hemel Hempstead to a large country house with an adjoining farm on the borders of Hertfordshire and Bedfordshire. My parents lived there until my father's death in 1980, following which my mother sold the house to a gentleman from the Middle East. The new owner, a playboy, remodelled the place from top to bottom, threw parties and entertained on a grand scale. A few years later, still relatively young, he was killed while flying a microlight plane in the United States. Long afterwards it emerged that he was the eldest half-brother of Osama Bin Laden, instigator of the terrorist attack on New York and Washington DC on 11th September 2001.

At seventeen, I was sent to Switzerland in a failed attempt to continue my education. It did have me skiing with reasonable competency, and there was one heart-stopping moment on a day trip to Gstaad when we girls, imperfect rebels from various parts of the world, were taken to tea in an exclusive hotel. Somebody noticed a celebrity in a distant corner, and a friend who had taken a spill on the slopes and broken her leg was up on her feet (the good one anyway), dragging me with her. "Come on," she begged. "I want a signature on my cast!" So the two of us, suddenly and uncharacteristically nervous, crossed the room and approached the table where the megastar sat. A moment later, perhaps taking pity on our obvious trepidation, and with barely a word spoken between us, Marlene Dietrich nodded assent, leant forward in her seat and signed the cast.

My travelling life, touring through many countries and based for extended periods in several of them, began in earnest when I was twenty-two. The age of majority was then twenty-one so it was not until after this milestone had passed that I could contemplate overseas travel without asking permission from higher authority. Undeterred by the fact that I had no funds and was alone, I accepted that live-in work would be essential and scoured the *Positions Vacant* of major newspapers for several months, looking and applying for jobs that included accommodation. At the time, visas were unnecessary to enter Commonwealth countries and comparatively easy to acquire for many others. After six months in Europe, I flew for the first time to work in the United States. For some years, my dream had been to visit North America, although I had no idea then that years later I would return and be based there for almost thirty years.

Coming to America

The intrepidness of youth –
cooking Cordon Bleu – off to see the world –
Oyster Bay and Manhattan – Bull Island

On the plane to New York with precious little cash but plenty of gall, I wanted to pinch myself. There I was, twenty-two going on twenty-three, and I'd landed a six-month job as a cook in America. In the hold were forty-four pounds of luggage including a paperback cookery tome and a few crudely typed recipes for dishes that I thought tasted well and might come in handy.

My mother was incredulous when I brandished the job offer. The more she thought about it, the more her voice rose until there came a final apoplectic cry: "But you can't cook!"

At the time I thought this unfair. It was not my fault that, together with my twin sister Mary, I was banned from the kitchen as a child and lacked practical experience. At the time it was thought we might get under the feet of those labouring there. Where one of us might have gained entry, two were double trouble so we were sent packing.

Fortunately, where my mother was a stickler for compliance ("Stay out of the kitchen please!"), dear Aida, our Portuguese cook, was less rigid. Sometimes we were curious to see what was being prepared, but most of the time there was the idea that a snack might alleviate boredom. Aida, a warm soul, either indulged us or pretended not to be watching as we raided the fridge or perused the larder.

When Aida rested during the afternoons, our mother sometimes experimented with new recipes (desserts in particular). Much as we wanted to watch over the bowl in which ingredients were mixed, we knew better than to try. On the plus side, if the recipe met with family approval, then Aida took notes in Portuguese and was left to concoct it in future. This of course opened the door to young rustlers.

In our teens we took a once-weekly cooking class at boarding school. I remember little about these lessons except that we made loaves of bread and perhaps a tart, and we always baked individual Christmas cakes to take home in December. The cake-making took place over several lessons and by the end of term I'd lost interest. It was icing the cake that drove me insane. Mary had patience and was clearly more talented. She iced with attention to detail and her cake had intricate latticework and was invariably commended when the cakes were judged. My attempt was considerably more haphazard. Not that I minded; I have never been partial to fruit cake, so by the time it came to icing I went for speed over care just to get it done.

My parents never made comments, at least not in my hearing, as to which cake looked or tasted better. However, this might have inspired my mother to consider whether I needed help in the culinary department. A couple of years later she thought to encourage my ability (or lack thereof) by giving me the gift of a one-week course at the London Cordon Bleu as a combined Christmas and birthday present. By then I was in my late teens and had my sights set on moving to the capital, so the gift was happily received.

The one-week course was actually Monday to Friday. Furthermore, at the London Cordon Bleu this meant just one dish cooked in the morning and one more in the afternoon. In all, a total of ten. Early each morning the demonstrator cooked the first dish while we students watched and listened. Then we made the same dish at individual counters with independent cooking hobs. The demonstration was accompanied by warnings to be neat and efficient and to clear up as we went along. When it came to our turn to cook, we were each supplied with ingredients and a recipe sheet, and the instructor walked around the room, doling out advice and overseeing progress. The afternoon session followed the same routine.

When the week was over, my father thought it would be great if, with my newly acquired skill, I cooked the family dinner one evening the following week. I was happy to oblige. Furthermore, the kitchen would be mine and mine alone. Aida had the evening off and my mother, suppressing a smile, let me get on with it.

The recipes from the Cordon Bleu all involved a lengthy list of ingredients; economy and cost were not discussed during the course. Not surprisingly, when I set about preparing to cook at home there were plenty of ingredients we didn't have, so these had to be furnished by a grocer who delivered twice a week. I cannot recall precisely what I cooked, but I think there might have been a chilled lemon soufflé for dessert. Happily, all went well and my parents were appreciative and encouraging. Much later I reflected on the fact that if they were being discreetly polite I was not aware of it, although I did note I was never asked to repeat the effort.

When I moved to London and began to flat-share, meals were on a tight budget and kept simple. Prepare in five minutes and eat in one minute. Eggs, cheese and bread formed the staple diet, hopefully augmented by men taking me out for better balanced meals.

It was a few years before my course at the Cordon Bleu truly came into its own. And did it how! Wanting to travel the world but with no cash in hand, I wrote a curriculum vitae aimed at gaining a residential position. In those days, well before the era of computers, work offers appeared in the columns of *The Times* and *The Lady* magazine. Eventually I landed a job in Provence, France, as an au pair for four months, working for a family originally from South Africa. The father in the family had just finished several years' working in London and, together with his wife and four children, was taking a break before returning home. They needed a young lady to accompany them to an artist's house they were renting in Menerbes, not far from Avignon. I supervised the two younger children and pitched in whenever required. It proved to be a perfect start to two years' travelling around the world and included some wonderful excursions along the Riviera.

Following France, I helped run two Greek villas catering to young English guests. It was there, while I was living on the island of Toulon, that I began making inroads into working in America. Between making an impostor of a *moussaka* or drinking *retsina*, I wrote to an American gentleman who, with his family, I had first met while on holiday in Scotland some years earlier. I included my dubious CV and a few weeks later received a reply although not from him. I later learnt that the American commuted weekdays by train from Long

Island into Manhattan and that it was on one of these journeys that he showed my letter to the wealthy lawyer seated beside him. On my CV I claimed that, among my accomplishments, I had completed a short course at the London Cordon Bleu. The lawyer read this and promptly wrote offering me a six-month position as cook, first at his home in Long Island and then on his quail shooting plantation off the coast of South Carolina.

I returned to London to prepare for this new position and brandished the lawyer's letter in front of my mother, who protested I was unqualified. In her eyes, a one-week course at the London Cordon Bleu didn't cut the mustard as far as being a professional cook was concerned. "This time you've really gone too far!" she exclaimed, knowing full well it would fall on deaf ears.

Of course I didn't see it her way. I was young and fearless, and what I didn't know couldn't hurt me. Call it the intrepidness of youth. Moreover, I was being offered the princely sum of US$100 a week, plus full board, so there was no chance I would reject such an exceptional offer.

Buoyed up with excitement, I shot to London, obtained a visa and bought my air ticket. Having accumulated no savings myself, I used almost the entire contents of a Post Office Savings Book given to me by my mother. She had arduously saved three-penny pieces (former currency before decimalisation) over many years and deposited them at the local Post Office into two savings books, one for me and one for Mary. These had been presented to us on our twenty-first birthdays and, while not specifically stated, the understanding was that we would keep them and by our own endeavours add to the amount contained therein. Well, once given, the contents were ours and as this was a moment of dire need and utmost priority, I had no qualms about spending it.

* * *

I flew to New York in early November, a few weeks before the annual American holiday of Thanksgiving. My future employer, Mr. Alfred Lee Loomis Jnr, was waiting for me in the Arrivals Hall at John F. Kennedy airport, and the first I saw of him was the top of his crew cut protruding above a large cardboard sign saying JULIA. Minutes later I was sitting in the rear of a chauffeur-driven limousine, with my new boss seated in front. We were on our way to a large white mansion in the elegant suburb of Oyster Bay on Long Island.

I wrote gleefully to my parents a few weeks later that my room had its own television set as well as a rocking chair. In those days, one television per family in Britain was the most anyone might expect and even that was considered a luxury. This beautiful American home seemed to have them dotted all over the place, including staff rooms. The rest of the house was furnished to dizzying heights, complete with hanging spoils from some big game shooting enterprise in Kenya a few years before. Among the trophies was a buffalo head and some elephant tusks, spoils that today might be shamefully retained in a cellar.

A couple of hours after arriving, and undaunted by jet lag, I was in the kitchen when Mrs. Loomis came to meet me. She was warmth and gentility personified. In her hand she had handwritten instructions on foolscap paper containing menus for the week ahead. Everything was noted from the corn beef hash for Monday's breakfast through to the hot cheese canapés to accompany Friday night's cocktails. I might have freaked out had I not already met Ida, the house manager, who assured me she would show me the ropes. She knew precisely how everything should be prepared and presented. As I soon discovered, she also knew how to salvage a disaster such as a curdling sauce for eggs Benedict. As a backup if Ida wasn't available, I resorted to my paperback cookbook carefully stowed in my bedside drawer. Fortunately, because the food was of the highest quality, much of it required relatively simple preparation.

The kitchen fridge held many different types of milk. At that time in Britain, milk was delivered in bottles with aluminium caps. Gold caps had thick cream on top, while silver and red had less or none at all. In America, the packaging was different and there was a much wider range including skimmed and semi skimmed-milk, both of which were then new to me.

Dear Mrs. Loomis, forever kind and generous, noted that I hadn't brought suitable clothes for cooking. I thought an apron would suffice but she knew better. "Oh but you don't want to get your pretty clothes dirty in the kitchen," she said, before announcing that I should accompany her on her next trip to Manhattan. So back in the limousine one morning and off we went into the city and my first visit to Bloomingdale's. There she bought me white overalls, a dirndl dress and blouse, petticoats, a white cardigan and two pairs of expensive flat shoes. I followed her around the store, watching wide-eyed as she launched into some Christmas shopping for her daughters. Without batting an eyelid, she paused at the handbag counter, bought eight or nine leather handbags by pointing to them on the shelves. After announcing a chosen colour for each, it was left to the assistant to arrange delivery.

Mr. Loomis continued commuting weekdays to Manhattan. On these mornings I was asked to place his breakfast down on the table whether he was seated or not. The train had precedence over a hot meal and he would bound downstairs the moment he was ready, gobble the lot in seconds and rush out to the chauffeur driven car waiting to take him to the station. He worked in Wall Street and, although a lawyer by profession, spent most of his time overseeing his considerable financial assets. He did admit to me, with a proud sparkle in his eyes, that he also made occasional visits for unspecified reasons to see the incumbent of the White House.

Mr. Loomis was a tall, large gentleman with a mischievous sense of humour. He adored his wife and regularly complimented her. For her part, Mrs. Loomis carefully watched her figure and if, as she said, her stomach protruded to the point that she could no longer read the scales at her feet, she cut back at lunch. At such times, and only during the week, she took a small glass of skimmed milk and a minuscule hamburger without bread.

After two weeks and several trips to Manhattan, I was told it was time to leave for the quail shooting plantation off the coast of South Carolina. Ida was staying behind with her husband to manage the Long Island home through the winter, but I was assured there would be others on the island to assist me. Thus I accompanied the Loomis' on the 15-hour train journey to Bluffton, South Carolina. From there we crossed by boat to Bull Island, a quail shooting plantation covering 2000 acres. On the island I was to live in a small bungalow, a two-minute walk from the main house.

For the first few hours after arriving, the whole place seemed like heaven on earth. The plantation was covered with palm trees and wild magnolias, and masses of camellias were blooming close to my new home. Long silvery strands of what was referred to as Spanish moss hung from the trees, giving shade and adding an air of serenity and calm. There were several other bungalows for staff as well as a large area reserved for dog kennels and stables. Twenty pointers, used in pairs to hunt quail, stayed in the kennels, along with two labradors trained for duck shooting. At least fifteen horses were housed in the stables, all having been transported from Tennessee along with two handlers.

Soon after arriving, I was taken on a tour of the island in an open jeep. Wild donkeys, turkeys, deer and duck were all around, along with some wild buffalo and zebra imported from a former island the family had owned. Large mounds of old oyster shells left by Native Americans years before lay here and there, together with little 'quail gardens' where the birds were reared before the start of the hunting season.

When I entered the kitchen to start work, I opened a mammoth fridge and stared nonplussed at a row of small, innocuous-looking bottles along the top rack inside the door. In size and shape they could have passed for vanilla essence or some other extract.

Delmar, the ageing plantation manager, was leaning against the door when I arrived. He watched as I inspected the bottles and grinned roguishly. "Why honey chil', dem's nothin' to worry your little head about. Dat's just de serum."

"The serum?" I asked puzzled.

"Case of dem snakes. Dem rattlers. De place is full of de rattlers."

He must have seen the look on my face because he couldn't help adding that alligators also lurked in the marshy terrain. "'Course most times dey don't come out till de spring." He raised his eyes and shrugged doubtfully.

It was then only autumn and we both knew my contract did not expire till the spring. I calculated with luck that I might only have snakes to contend with, but Delmar was not reassuring.

"Just keep to dem tracks," he warned bluntly. "Last year dey shot one dat long." He gestured expansively with his hands along the kitchen wall.

"Really?" I said trying to sound unaffected. In fact I was more than a little disquieted and in the months ahead it was this conversation that, more than anything, influenced me to ride round the island rather than walk.

Certainly it was not the most encouraging start to life on Bull Island. I already had enough worries with an increased workload. Fortunately, in place of Ida, there was now Pearl, a veritable southern treasure who had worked on the plantation for many years. Like Ida, she knew a good deal more about cooking than I did but was too kind to embarrass me. The only time she mildly chastised me was when I tried to hand a china plate containing some ham through a window to an elderly African American worker outside. It was a holiday weekend and the old man had been left on the island to work alone. He was not permitted in the kitchen and when Pearl saw what I was doing, she abruptly took the plate from my hands, removed the cutlery and slipped the ham on to a paper plate. The civil rights struggles of the '60s were far from over in the south.

Most of the food was prepacked, tinned or frozen and sent over by speedboat from the mainland several times a week. What Pearl didn't know about the preparation, the wrapper usually did. Also, in addition to my own book, there was a drawer full of American cookery books offering advice.

As it turned out, the hardest part of my work had little to do with the actual preparation of food. Arranging the dining-room table was more of a headache than whisking lumps out of a white sauce. With some fifteen dinner services to choose from, three cupboards full of cut glasses, and drawers full of linen napkins, determining which combination to use was an art in itself. Some of the dinner services were also considered too valuable to eat from. These hand-painted heirlooms were only used for the table setting before the meal began. If the first course was soup, then the individual tureen was laid on top of the priceless plate and, when the course was over, both removed. Money, it would seem, can buy you out of one set of problems, but land you with another.

When I was free in the afternoons, I sometimes rode one of the horses through the plantation. I took a fancy to a Tennessee walking horse called Sonny, and together we made our way through the palm trees to the northernmost tip of the island. Happily, neither Sonny nor I were ever confronted by a rattlesnake or an alligator. The only snake to appear while I was there was shot by Mr. Loomis. According to Delmar, it was an insignificant little thing with a contemptible eighteen rattles. Snakes or no snakes, though, there was something very splendid about sitting on Sonny as he gambolled along on those warm afternoons, his legs kicking out in the famous Tennessee trot, a great lolloping side to side gait, so smooth to ride. Dem rattlers, I used to tell myself, could never spoil that.

The Thanksgiving holiday kept me busy in the kitchen. There were two turkeys to be cooked, one for the Loomis family and their guests, and one for the staff. The Loomis's had their turkey boiled in a muslin cloth and served with oysters in a white sauce. Of the side dishes, one was new to me. It was mashed sweet potato beneath a marshmallow topping, the top browned under the grill. Pearl helped with this as well as taking over the preparation of the staff turkey, which was dissected, breaded and deep fried.

Every weekend there was an increasing number of guests and eventually Mr. Loomis brought in a young Irish chef. By this time I was more than happy to let Johnnie take over and stood by as his assistant. At weekends, when he had guests, Mr. Loomis would call me into the lounge after dinner and introduce me to his guests as his English Cordon Bleu cook. At this time English secretaries were considered *de rigueur* in America, and perhaps he thought he had gone one better with an English cook. In any case I always carried a box of cigars to offer his guests while retaining a particularly special cigar (illicit contraband from Cuba) in my overall pocket. As I passed by his place at the table, he surreptitiously removed his own cigar.

Mrs. Loomis's generosity knew no bounds and extended to all staff at Christmas. I was presented with four beautiful gifts, and to top them off Mr. Loomis then handed me an envelope containing a bonus of $100.

One evening before they returned to New York in early spring, I was called into the lounge after dinner. I still had a month to go before my contract expired but they determined, to my amazement, that this last month was for me to spend as I wished. They had already been away once before and given me two weeks off, so another month left me speechless. During the first two weeks, I had gone south by Greyhound bus seeing Georgia and Florida as well as visiting a cousin in the Bahamas. Now they determined that, from the following week, I was to become their (paid) guest! Furthermore, I could stay at any one of their homes which included a house in Boston, their home in Oyster Bay, an apartment in Manhattan, and the island plantation. I chose to spend a week in the Manhattan apartment, from where I toured the city and visited Washington DC.

Before I left New York, Mr. Loomis took me to the Oyster Bay shipyard to see the 12-metre yacht 'Northern Light' that he had been given by his father as a 24th birthday present. Years later, and then owned by the Greek shipping tycoon, Stavropol Niarchos, the yacht was involved in that most prestigious of sailing races, the America's Cup.

From New York I flew to Detroit for a weekend and then on to California and a coach tour down the coast from San Francisco to Los Angeles. Finally, I flew to Honolulu for a few days before leaving the United States and heading on to Australia. By the time I left America, I still had a great deal more cash in my pocket than I had ever had in my British Post Office Savings account. And one *short* course at the London Cordon Bleu had paid for itself many times over!

Food Follies

When a man cooks – the French and their cuisine –
shortcuts, alcohol and etiquette – taking a man to dinner

Over time I have cooked for a number of men who preferred different types of cuisine. If they took me out to dinner, I felt obliged at one time or another to reciprocate. Among these was an American of Italian descent who loved pasta; a Frenchman who purported to eat anything; and a diabetic for whom I bought a special recipe book and attempted to meet his needs without forfeiting flavour. There was another gentleman who preferred Middle Eastern cuisine and finally an Englishman who suggested that I shop for ingredients but best leave the cooking to him.

Let's begin with this latter gentleman. At the time we were living together in a lovely flat in Sydney, Australia, overlooking the harbour. I spent my days struggling to get published while he organised a fleet of red mini skirted young ladies selling real estate on the city's north shore. Every morning before he left, he determined what we would have for dinner and left me to buy the ingredients. Come evening, he rushed home from work, changed into casual gear and, pausing only at the bar, headed for the kitchen. It went without saying that I was his *sous* chef, with the added responsibility of cleaning up when the meal was over. This of course gave him carte blanche to use as many pots and pans as he wished and, when he sat back with a cigar after dinner, I was left to repair a kitchen that looked as if a hurricane had blown through.

One evening he announced he was cooking brown rice as an accompaniment to a type of beef ragout. You might think this sounds simple, but then you haven't seen the recipe for the rice. Male devotees of the kitchen tend not to cook ordinary dishes and this was no ordinary rice. I already had the basic ingredients such as bay leaves, turmeric, peppercorns and olive oil but I was short, among other things, of pure Spanish saffron, cumin seed, mace and a stick of green ginger. In my experience, men are inclined to throw economy out of the window when they take charge of the kitchen. I do admit, however, that after arduous preparation, the rice tasted excellent. The only problem was that he cooked enough to feed an army and much of it was wasted.

The problems of living with a man who thinks he's a great cook is second only to marrying into a family who really *are* great cooks. I once had two sisters-in-law who were superb at preparing all manner of meals. They never failed. To my amazement I watched one of them host a Sunday brunch and serve up soft poached eggs on top of marinated artichoke hearts to more than twenty guests. She weaved through the throng, chatting away, and yet still managed to serve up soft eggs in perfect condition. She too could cook exquisite rice, only hers contained slivers of sour cherries and almonds. My husband saw how impressed I was and warned against competing. Frankly, I couldn't have, even if I had a mind to.

Thirty years later the Frenchman took one look at my minute London kitchen and determined never to enter it himself. He professed to eat anything and sat back expectantly, content with a glass of wine. While I regard French cuisine as among the best in the world, I also accept that the French regard meals as the highlight of their day. To them food is almost a form of communion, so it goes without saying that they are picky and expect the best as they know it. Dare I add here that in the past a few elite Frenchmen, a leading politician in particular, have been a tad critical of other cuisines, particularly British? While there is nothing wrong with frogs' legs, snails in garlic or tartiflette, try suggesting to the French that they sample toad-in-the-hole, sausage rolls or haggis, and they look aghast. Part of it might be in the presentation for which the French have a talent, but it might also have something to do with the ingredients. Not that the French are sticklers for healthy components. The amount of cream and butter they cram into some of their dishes is enough to make a nutritionist faint.

But I digress. Back to the Frenchman and my efforts to please. Early in our relationship, I searched to provide the best meals without torturing myself in their preparation. Hoping to impress, I raced to a supermarket one day having learnt that lobster tails were on sale. I thought these would please him and returned triumphantly with two tails wrapped in paper which I popped straight in the fridge. Regrettably, I never examined them first. When the time came to serve the entrée, I whipped them out of the paper and placed them on plates. I thought they looked a tad pale but it wasn't until after the requisite *'Bon Appétit!'*, and I sunk my fork into mine, that I realised they were raw. Unfortunately I had mistakenly assumed they were sold cooked. This led to a hoot of mirth from the Frenchman, who grabbed his phone, snapped a photo and, to my chagrin, emailed it *tout de suite* to his brothers.

Fortunately, one of his siblings, the most compassionate of the three, had the goodness to write back "Shit happens". There followed an extended wine break while I boiled the little buggers and the meal continued.

I persevered over time and the same gentleman had the grace to say that my culinary skills had improved. I knew, however, that it was not necessarily because I cooked any better, but rather that I had become attuned to his likes and dislikes. His claim to eat anything was clearly exaggerated; the foods he disdained were curry, game, crab, lambs' kidneys (only veal would do) and certain vegetables, including broccoli. Moreover, he would only eat lamb in a restaurant and was disappointed at having fish served on the bone.

In a further endeavour to please him, I began studying French. I took lessons at home before signing on for a two-week stint at a French school in Nice. While I was there I picked up an amusing little hand-painted tile in the market. The tile portrayed a cartoon figure of a buxom lady at work in her kitchen with a rolling pin in hand. The caption beneath the lady read: *"C'est ici qu'habite la meilleure cuisinière du monde"* (here lives the best cook in the world). I hung the tile outside my front door before my friend arrived for dinner. I accept this was tempting a response and sure enough, the moment he arrived, his phone re-emerged and a new photo emailed to his family. This time, if there were comments, I was spared hearing them.

What the Frenchman never knew was that I had the last laugh. Aware that he had reservations about British cuisine, I determined to serve him a meal which, if he knew what it was, he would refuse even to sample. One evening I told him we were having 'pulled pork' for dinner and, back turned, slit a cooked pork haggis and scooped some onto two plates. Surprise, surprise, he enjoyed it so much he asked for more. Considering that he had earlier disdained the dish as being too inferior for his exalted palate, it was my turn to feel smug.

Over years, and knowing my shortcomings, I have learnt to keep my culinary efforts simple. For me there are more interesting things to do and, being practical, I can't help considering how fast a meal is consumed compared to the expenditure of time and energy required to produce it. I have, however, learnt that providing plenty to drink may divert attention from the food, sometimes with amusing results. I once had a guest come to dinner, drink copiously and be wickedly conned by a flower. At the time I had an obsession with indoor plants; they were suspended in bright red holders from my living-room ceiling; cascaded out of plant boxes fixed to the wall; and grew in pots along the windowsill. Unfortunately, because the room had only brief spells of sunlight, none of the plants flowered. One year, at Easter, I was given a chocolate egg wrapped in cellophane with a jaunty, albeit fake, flower pinned on top. The flower was made from some type of starched material and vaguely resembled a camellia. Having eaten the egg, I plucked the flower from the wrapping and wistfully attached it to a plant suspended from the ceiling. A fortnight later a few friends came for dinner and, when the meal was over, they sat back enjoying cognac after several bottles of wine. As they grew mellow, someone pointed out that one of my plants had finally bloomed and they focused blurry attention on the camellia. One guest, suddenly moved, rose from his seat and, swaying gently, advanced towards the flower. He stared at it enrapt before exclaiming at length: "Isn't nature wonderful?" Those less inebriated laughed and the incident signalled the close of a happy evening. Amid so much mirth, the meal was overlooked.

Another dinner backfired when I cut short the preparation. I couldn't face making a dessert so I pared down the menu by retrieving a packet mix from the back of a cupboard. I whipped up a cheesecake in no time and spent the afternoon reading a book. Not surprisingly, when ideals blow out the window, hypocrisy tends to fly in. Questioned about the dessert, I reeled off the list of ingredients from the side of the packet, carefully omitting those that smacked of commercialism. I vented a lovely spiel about blending this and beating that which wasn't so much an untruth as exaggerating a tad. Although my guests thought the dessert was excellent, I didn't quite get away with it. Pride took a tumble when someone proffered what he assumed to be the ultimate compliment and told me it was the best dessert I had ever made.

These days I tend to eat out rather than entertain at home. When I was young and growing up in the country, the only time I was taken to a restaurant was the night before I was bundled off to a new term at boarding school. Where I lived, there were neither coffee shops nor bistros, so eating out was a special event and usually involved a trip to London. Needless to say, the first such outing came with the inevitable lecture on not choosing the most expensive item on the menu. Similarly there could be no gobbling and no asking for more than I could manage without making myself ill. There was instruction on the use of cutlery, how much should be pushed on the back of a fork, and the use of a napkin. In retrospect, probably the best lesson was appreciation and courtesy towards those who provided the meal.

Having learnt table etiquette in Britain, I later discovered variations elsewhere. In the United States there were occasions when I saw young people, usually men, snuffling at the trough for prizes or free meals. In certain eating establishments, contests were a way to attract custom and there were always plenty of participants willing to gobble pies, gulp oysters or struggle through a mountain of doughnuts at breakneck speed, all for a cash reward.

In Texas I once witnessed an eating marathon open to all-comers, inviting guests to try for a free meal. There were no prizes and no coveted titles for those who succeeded. The contest was in the form of a bet between management and guest. If the patron failed to consume every morsel placed before him (or her), he would be penalised. If he managed to eat the entire feast, the meal was free. By offering such a meal, the restaurant cunningly lured not only those ravenous enough to take up the challenge but many who simply wanted to observe.

Details and rules were posted at the door. The free dinner consisted of a 72oz steak (just over 2kg), a shrimp cocktail, one baked potato, a tossed salad, and a roll with butter. For aspiring competitors there was a clear set of rules: the entire meal had to be consumed in one hour and the time had to be recorded by a waitress or waiter. Once the meal was begun, an entrant was not permitted to leave the table until it was finished and, while it was not mandatory to eat the fat, this had to be judged by the server. Finally, if any part of the meal was left over after the time limit had expired, you lost. The penalty for losing – and the proprietors were strict about this – was, in today's value, close to US$70. The dinner was particularly popular with local cowboys who arrived in groups and tackled the meal with gusto. I went in one evening and, while eating a lean grain fed steak served with pinto beans in a pungent garlic sauce, watched seven hefty cowboys attempt the free dinner. Six ploughed happily through the lot, apparently without ill effect. The seventh was forced to retire and pay the penalty.

Despite early training with table manners, I've had at least one eating disaster of my own. My father, a stickler for etiquette, was fortunately not around to see it. As part of his work, he was obliged to take an annual overseas trip and having once been conned into eating frogs' legs in India (he was told they were chicken), he became similarly suspicious of alien cuisines and how to consume them.

My comeuppance came after working in Mongolia. Due to the less than reliable flight schedule from Ulaan Baatar (often due to weather), I booked a two-night layover in Beijing to ensure that I caught my next flight to Los Angeles and on home to Florida. As it happened, there were no delays or cancellations, and I arrived in Beijing with almost two days to spare before the next leg of the journey. I duly booked myself into a Chinese hotel at the airport and prepared to wait out the interim. In the hotel the receptionist spoke little English, but I made her understand that I would like breakfast both days. On entering the restaurant the first morning, I sized up what was on offer at the buffet and promptly regretted requesting the meal. The array of strange seaweed concoctions and noodles was unappealing and there was little else on offer. Feeling desperate, I suddenly spotted a chef standing behind a frying pan and a hot plate with a pile of eggs on the side. I headed straight over and with a plate in hand and two fingers raised, he understood that I would like two cooked eggs. It seemed that fried was the only style but by then I wasn't particular.

Once the eggs were cooked, he slid them silently onto my outstretched plate. By then I had already noticed that it was the type of buffet where you collected utensils, in this case chopsticks, from a side table close to the seaweed. I quickly selected a pair and withdrew to a corner table well away from the crowd. Being the only non-Chinese in the room, I felt a little conspicuous.

The problem came when I tried to cut and consume the eggs with chopsticks. They kept slithering around out of reach. When a piece was tenuously gripped between the sticks, getting it up and into my mouth was another hassle. I just hoped nobody was observing because, and thank God for paper napkins, it couldn't have been a pretty sight.

Next morning, and better prepared, I copied the Chinese who took bowls instead of plates. I watched as they took food and how they ate. They held the bowl close to their faces before scooping up the seaweed with chopsticks and shovelling it into their mouths with dexterity born of practice. What they did, so could I...or so I thought. I duly ordered two more eggs, had them placed in a bowl, and went to collect my chopsticks. Unbeknown to me, and clear proof the Chinese are hot with intelligence, I realised that I had been observed the day before. Beside the pile of chopsticks now rested a single set of cutlery, old and bent out of shape. I politely gathered up some chopsticks and the cutlery, and sat down at a vacant table, acutely aware I was being watched. First I tried eating with the chopsticks, hoping any observers, whoever and wherever they were, would note with approval that I was following local tradition and determined to eat as they did. Unfortunately, I was no more successful eating fried eggs from a bowl than from a plate, so I soon gave up and resorted to using the cutlery.

Another time I was relieved of a culinary dilemma by an enterprising carpenter. Working in a ski motel in the Snowy Mountains between Sydney and Melbourne, a problem arose when, in a fit of pique and after an argument with the manager, the chef upped and left. Two coach loads of skiers had arrived that morning and were expected back from the slopes for dinner at seven. Confronting the crisis, the manageress allotted tasks and I (general factotum) was told to prepare and cook a tray of small chickens as part of a new very short menu. Worse still, amid the scurry of activity, it was discovered the chef had pilfered the best knives on his way out.

The skiers appeared in the bar before entering the restaurant, just as I brought the chickens out of the oven. Each bird had to be split in two, but the one surviving bread knife clearly wasn't up to the task. The German housekeeper, normally full of advice, left the staff table and studied the situation. As she sniffed disdainfully, the waitresses began to panic. What to do? There was not a good knife in sight and the skiers were starving.

It was Mike, a New Zealander and the resident carpenter, who ambled over and sized up the situation. Without a word he left the kitchen, returning two minutes later with an unwieldy saw covered in sawdust. The housekeeper looked appalled, shaking her head in disbelief and returning po-faced to the staff table. Undaunted, Mike took the ungainly implement to the sink and began scrupulously washing it. Soon afterwards he sawed down the breastbone of thirty chickens, calmly loading half to a plate. While his actions wouldn't pass health regulations then or today, he got the job done. The waitresses grabbed the plates and the skiers were fed. There were no dire consequences, save perhaps a hangover or two, and they all returned to the slopes early next morning.

Lastly to an unforgettable restaurant dinner when I was in my late twenties. After a few years of submitting work to newspapers, journals and literary awards, I was finally getting published on a regular basis. I used to type out manuscripts, ranging from newspaper articles to short fiction, and mail them from the nearest post office, always including a stamped addressed envelope for their return. At any one time, I would have up to twenty manuscripts, ranging from travel pieces to short stories, sent to editors. This way I reasoned that if one or even two were rejected the same day, I had others out with a chance. Every morning I heard the postman's whistle as he progressed down the street and would hotfoot it to my mailbox, checking for contracts. When a submission was rejected, I inspected the condition of the manuscript. Coffee stains, pencil marks, ink blots or deeply folded corners all meant the work needed retyping but if the manuscript was clean and presentable, I could send it out again. My little red typewriter took a beating but soldiered on month after month, year after year. Eventually I gained an established spot on the back page of a national newspaper and cheques began arriving on a regular basis.

During this protracted endeavour, my first husband, Paul, had supported and encouraged me through thick and thin. I knew it was fitting, therefore, to host him to dinner as a small token of thanks. There was also, I admit, a certain amount of cachet in being able to say: 'This time it's on me.'

Flushed with goodwill, I told him we would dine at an exclusive restaurant close to home. He protested at the extravagance but was clearly pleased so I forged ahead and made the reservation. When the evening arrived, he insisted on asking one last time if I was absolutely sure I wanted to go, to which I endeavoured to look insulted and dismissed him with an airy wave of the hand.

Inside the restaurant, he refused a predinner drink, preferring to wait and have wine with the meal. I pressed him but he wouldn't hear of it. I assured him that when I said he could have whatever he wanted, I meant it. This time he smiled benevolently and settled down to study the menu. By the time the waiter arrived, he still hadn't made up his mind so I gave my order and sat back patiently. When he finally spoke, his lips barely moved yet the words emerged with exceptional clarity: "I'll have the Russian caviar followed by the salmon."

Of course I had noticed the caviar but not seriously, if you know what I mean. I glanced down the menu, trying not to make it look obvious. The waiter bowed reverently and streaked for the kitchen. Not for the world would I have shown alarm. "How lovely!" I exclaimed. "I know you'll love it. Can I try a smidgen?"

"Certainly not," came the retort. "If you wanted some, you should have asked for it."

I never said a word, just smiled again and pretended it was an amusing little joke. When the caviar arrived in a tiny glass bowl perched on a plush silver goblet full of crushed ice, and accompanied by a small bowl of mashed egg and a plate of toast, it certainly looked expensive. My own sea scallops seemed vastly inferior by comparison.

"This is excellent!" he exclaimed, specks of the precious crushed roe seeping blackly from his mouth. "This really is good!"

Suddenly it was all worthwhile and suffuse with the pleasure of giving, I wanted to blurt out that he should have some more but just managed to prevent myself. Who wants to be vulgar?

Unfortunately his delight was short-lived because we still had no wine. He glared round in dismay, his lips changing rapidly to a twitching purplish colour. When the wine list finally arrived, I turned away. At the time I thought there were still a few things a lady shouldn't do and choosing the wine was one of them. Today I feel far less subservient.

"Champagne!" I cried delighted, watching as the bucket was set in position and the cork gently removed. "French champagne," I was informed with relish. "Moët et Chandon."

I chastised myself for attempting some mental arithmetic; tomorrow would take care of itself. When he finished eating, I asked if he would like a liqueur and his eyes lit up with glee. "A cognac," he told the waiter. "The best please. And please make it a double."

When he slipped out for a couple of minutes, I pondered whether to suggest he top the lot off with a cigar. It was easier to concern myself with that than consider how many hours' work it would take to make up the cost.

In all, the meal took three hours. When I went to ask for the bill, he reached out and stopped me. "I've signed for it," he said quietly, smiling slightly. "And I won't hear another word."

Later I bought him a gift – but it was wonderful to know the age of chivalry was not dead.

Eleven Seconds

Flying Aeroflot – earthquake –
Hotel Armenia – television presenter

Shortly before the end of the Cold War, I flew regularly on Aeroflot from Moscow to Yerevan, capital of Armenia. At the time it was the only way from the West to reach the tiny Soviet Socialist Republic lying south of the Caucasus mountains east of Turkey.

More than thirty years have passed, but I well remember these flights and the hassle to board and claim a seat. Planes were invariably overbooked and allocation of boarding cards for most travellers was, to say the least, haphazard. Because I was a foreigner I had an In-Tourist ticket which helped ensure I had a seat but in no way guaranteed one. Moreover, foreigners were regarded with suspicion and I looked obviously alien.

Air hostesses, as they were then referred to, moved in to arbitrate disputes. Frequently, those unfortunate souls who missed out during the game of musical chairs, were obliged to disembark and forced to wait for another flight, possibly days later. There was no safety procedure, not even an explanatory card held aloft or placed in the seat pocket in front. Seatbelts, if there were any, were often faulty and there were no overhead reading lights or air-conditioning. The toilets, which were little more than seatless caverns, had neither water nor soap. With such a paucity of amenities, I had the disquieting thought that there might also be no oxygen masks.

Sometimes I had a guide to accompany me onto the plane. This was permitted for foreigners, perhaps with the aid of a bribe. I remember one guide saw me into my seat by the window before instructing strictly and repeatedly that I never leave it. "Look out of the window but DON'T MOVE!" he implored me. When I queried why, I learnt that members of the KGB were about to board and they would expect to have seats. Not surprisingly, when these invidious travellers arrived, a hush descended. Glancing round, I noticed almost every passenger was staring out of the nearest window! Once it was clear that nobody was prepared to sacrifice their seat, these men then proceeded to stand in the aisle and strap hang for the duration of the three hour flight, holding onto overhead lockers during turbulence.

Pilots were rarely heard from and seldom seen. The air hostesses sat chatting together and issued no instructions. Passengers took it upon themselves to determine when, after take-off, it was safe to rise from their seats. At this point they would retrieve goods from overhead lockers, in particular newspaper wrapped parcels carefully stowed before take-off.

A picnic ensued. Within minutes the smell of brine, garlic and barbecued meat permeated the entire cabin. I once sat close to a man who spent several minutes attempting to prise the lid from a jar of pickled onions wedged between his knees. Once open, and to the amusement of those sitting around him, he tried unsuccessfully to extricate an onion with his fingers. Restricted by the narrow neck of the jar, the onions kept sliding round out of reach but eventually, with the aid of a fork, he stabbed one and withdrew it triumphantly, brandishing it aloft to a round of applause.

Hard-boiled eggs were peeled, nuts shelled and cake sliced. Everyone had plenty of bread. The pungent smell of garlic, along with spiced sausage and cooked meat, grew stronger. As food was passed around, there was a general ambiance of bonhomie. With smiles and thanks, I politely declined a pickled onion.

The refreshing camaraderie among passengers, almost all Armenian, contrasted with the hostesses' disinterest. They came down the aisle with small rattling trolleys, offering some rancid green cordial in plastic cups and selling miniature gobstoppers and sugared fruit slices. Dressed in ill-fitting pinafores with cheap black shoes, their indifferent presentation was mirrored in their demeanour. They seemed dispirited, spoke only Russian and exhibited not the slightest enthusiasm, feigned or otherwise.

On one flight, I watched a red setter trot up and down the aisle hoovering up scraps of meat and other tasty morsels. Dogs, it seemed, required neither seat nor crate, and could wander at will through the cabin. Either that or this particular canine had human friends in high places.

But perhaps the most telling detail of flying Aeroflot to and from Armenia came at the end of the flight. At the time it was not surprising that the airline had one of the worst safety records in the world. When the flight landed and the plane safely touched down, some of the older ladies, abandoning Communist principles, gratefully crossed themselves.

* * *

Eleven seconds changed every Armenian's life forever but at the time I had no idea they would also change mine.

The earthquake happened on 7th December, 1988. I was then living happily in New York with my second husband, Loris, a composer and conductor of Armenian descent. We were watching the news and saw how the earthquake, registering 6.9 on the Richter scale, had devastated a large swathe of Armenia, flattening several cities and towns. At the time of the disaster, Soviet President Mikhail Gorbachev was in New York, meeting with US President Ronald Reagan to forge closer relations with the West. Gorbachev cut short his visit and returned to Moscow to lead the recovery effort.

In the days that followed we saw reports of volunteer teams from many countries arriving to help. Rescue workers, some with dogs, others with high-tech equipment such as heat-seeking cameras or infrared detectors, searched through the rubble. Medical teams arrived to assess injuries and arrange for some of the victims to be airlifted to hospitals overseas for specialist attention. The earthquake could not have occurred at a worse time of year. Landlocked and poor, Armenia is a mountainous land with long cold winters and snow covering the country for months at a time.

Loris determined to help in whatever way he could and flew to Armenia on a preliminary visit. On his return he announced we would go and live in Yerevan so that he could rebuild the national orchestra in an effort to restore local culture and boost morale. I packed up our New York apartment and sent some of our possessions to London and some to Armenia. It was several months after the earthquake before I arrived to live in Yerevan, yet evidence of the horror was all around. Adding to the problems was the housing shortage throughout the country. There had been too few homes before the earthquake but now homeless people poured into the capital moving in with relatives and friends.

When I visited the stricken area northwest of Yerevan, streets remained a quagmire, mud churned up by the constant tracking of heavy vehicles still trying to clear the debris. Other trucks were transporting fresh building materials to cleared sites ready for construction. Where front walls of apartment buildings had been torn away, I looked into what had once been a bedroom or a lounge. Strips of wallpaper floated in the breeze. From below I wondered who had lived there. What had they eaten that last morning at breakfast before the first tremor ripped through their home and sent it crashing into those below?

Rapidly constructed shanty huts had sprung up wherever space could be found. Made out of corrugated iron, they had neither electricity nor running water. People were warned it could take five years before proper accommodation would be found for them. In the meantime I watched people trudging to the nearest pump to fill buckets with water.

During my visit local dignitaries insisted on serving a meal on a long makeshift table. Tiny birds, probably sparrows, were given one to each person. It was all there was to offer but Armenian tradition insists a guest is God's messenger and I and a few volunteers were honoured accordingly.

The Deputy Mayor explained how the first tremor was felt shortly before 11am in his city of Leninakan. Modern apartment blocks, some nine storeys high and cheaply constructed, immediately collapsed. Schools, smaller but no less vulnerable, disappeared amid clouds of dust and rubble. Only the older government buildings, built of sturdier material, fared any better. Almost at once, overhead power lines exploded, fires broke out and darkness descended. Those who survived uninjured, many of them men who were working in the government buildings, ran into the streets searching for their cars, desperate to check their families were safe and to collect children from school. Traffic jams followed, adding to the chaos.

Leninakan, once home to 300,000 people, was 80% destroyed while the small town of Spitak, close to the earthquake's epicentre, ceased to exist. Thousands were trapped in the debris and more than half a million were left homeless. Bodies lay deep beneath the rubble for weeks. The precise number of those who perished will never be known but estimates have reached 50,000. In time the dead were buried, many in unmarked graves along a hillside.

Towards the end of the meal, those officials who were present passed round precious faded photos of their families including loved ones they had lost. They themselves were past tears and it was the rest of us who shed them as we looked at a photo of a happy family of whom only the father now remained, or listened as one man told how his wife had been so mentally affected by the loss of her children and relatives that she had entered a sanitarium.

* * *

Yerevan, the Armenian capital, was thankfully unaffected by the earthquake. It became the centre from which much of the recovery effort was organised and into which hundreds of relief workers and volunteers came from around the world.

I arrived late one evening to stay in the aptly named Hotel Armenia, arguably the best hotel in the city at the time, and overlooking the main square. Loris had arrived weeks before me and was already hard at work in his new position as Principal Conductor of the Armenian Philharmonic Orchestra.

A guide had accompanied me from the airport and took me to the hotel where each floor was watched over by a lady sitting behind a desk close to the lift. Seda was the dear middle-aged lady waiting to greet me on my floor. The moment she saw me she grabbed some keys from her desk and led the way, sailing down the main corridor, matron of her domain. Seda spoke no English, but her warmth burst through the language barrier and embraced me like a long lost sister. We conversed in mime and smiles.

Our room, or should I say suite (it was large but certainly not opulent) had high ceilings and low windows with deep sills. The decor was drab and old. Two thin brown curtains and a torn net drape hung in front of the windows although, as I discovered next morning, the light streamed in regardless. Our single beds were sectioned off from the rest of the room by a tired red curtain. The floor was covered in a brown threadbare carpet and, where the seams separated, strands of fibre revealed the floorboards which were noticeably uneven and creaked loudly.

My guide had given me a posy of red roses, and when Seda saw these she went hurrying off to find a vase. On her return, arms full, she had clean towels and a minuscule piece of orange soap in one hand together with a small vase with the roses. In her other hand she carried a little tray bearing a tiny cup of thick black coffee and a further glass of the overly sweet cordial I had been offered on the plane.

In the bathroom there was a large antiquated bath, heavily stained, while the basin had a hairline crack extending from beneath a tap all the way to the drain. Above the basin, a glass shelf had been badly erected with the glass tilting at such an angle nothing could rest on it. When I turned on the taps, a great gurgling rumble emanated from somewhere behind the wall. The pending rush of approaching water veered closer and I stepped back tentatively. The taps shook with the force of compressed air until finally water exploded forth in great spluttering bursts, farting rudely as it came. The water was the colour of strongly brewed tea.

I was already well travelled by then and knew there were no surprises, good or bad, only discovery. Even the small amount of rough grey toilet paper did not deter me. I would, admittedly, have liked a plug for both the basin and the bath but these too were missing. However, if I could not take a bath, I could at least shower. Resting in a cradle above the bath taps was a shower head. This time, as I gingerly turned on the taps, wary of a new outburst, the water flowed noiselessly, the brownish colour quickly clearing. Now the only problem was the temperature; both taps produced ice-cold water. Fortunately, next morning the water ran warm and I learnt that unless it was cut off completely, as sometimes happened, I could expect warm water throughout the day.

In the following months I exterminated a number of cockroaches but was grateful our room was not infested with mice. An Irish nurse living on a lower floor and volunteering in a local hospital was not so lucky. Undeterred, she had the good sense to take the invasion in her stride, going so far as to laughingly chalk up 'kills' on the back of her door each time a rodent was caught in a trap.

If this sounds like a somewhat disheartening start to life in Armenia, what I witnessed my first morning at breakfast was in direct contrast. Not only was it illuminating but entertaining in more ways than one.

Although the hotel restaurant was as drab as my room, the need for refurbishment paled into insignificance beside the activity and commotion within. Waiters in plain grey suits moved between tables, presiding over the room with an air of indifference and obvious assurance. Few bothered to write down orders, preferring to commit them to memory or bring whatever was available. As I soon discovered, they were not only well-educated, they were entrepreneurs. It seemed their work was not simply to serve food, but to forge introductions between guests, some of whom were Armenians visiting from the diaspora, and others foreigners working for relief organisations.

When necessary the waiters would cross the entire length of the restaurant to convey introductions between guests. This was accomplished by way of handwritten notes, a whisper in the ear or, very occasionally, name cards. Whichever form of introduction was employed, once the waiter's role was done and a gratuity earned, it was left to the guests to follow up the introduction. As guests then passed to and fro between tables, they added to the general hullabaloo.

Most of the waiters smoked and did not conceal the habit. Their one concession was before serving food to rest cigarettes on a ledge by doors leading into and out of the kitchen. At times up to six cigarettes could be seen on this ledge, the lit ends protruding perilously over the edge.

If they felt so inclined, waiters would pull up a chair and sit down to chat with guests. I remember one morning, after Loris had conducted a concert the previous evening, a waiter pulled up a chair, sat at our table and without so much as a by-your-leave launched into intense discussion with him. Unable to understand, I sat silently observing. Once the waiter left, I was curious to know what they had talked about. "He wanted to discuss my interpretation of the Third Movement of the Shostakovich Symphony last night," I was told. My husband was inordinately proud of his people and there was no hint of surprise.

Despite the restaurant's austere appearance, the commotion within was invariably animated. The only people who remained detached from the excitement were some older ladies employed to clear and reset the tables. They wore aprons over their blouses and pushed around ungainly trolleys. These rattled and squeaked, further contributing to the hustle and bustle.

And for my first breakfast? Some warm meat-filled pancakes, savoury and very tasty.

* * *

I first worked at a local school teaching English and rewriting English texts. Most of the students already spoke Armenian and Russian but with the coming of political change (*Glasnost* and *Perestroika*, openness and reform) many looked forward to travelling with their families to the West.

Every morning I left Hotel Armenia and crossed the main square. I passed a tall grey authoritarian statue of Lenin, plus numerous relief trucks waiting to be loaded with supplies for the area affected by the earthquake. Down the side street leading to the Pedagogical Institute, hawkers sat by the side of the road selling everything from cheap disposable brands of razors to a few packets of chewing gum. Shoe menders worked in cramped kiosks and old men squatted beside ancient T-bar weighing scales or peddled cigarettes. The shops were no more inspiring and sometimes nearly empty. I once looked in a draper's shop and saw some plastic bags on one shelf, a handful of combs on another, and a few strands of beads and diamanté hair clips on a third. Nothing else.

Shopping involved queues in all seasons. When word spread that eggs or some other vital commodity were suddenly available in one of the few food shops, women rushed out and waited for hours. In winter, if they were lucky enough to buy some, they had to negotiate icy footpaths (no sand or salt) while balancing an open tray of eggs in one hand. Fruit and vegetables were bottled during the summer to last through the winter.

Crossing streets was a hazard to be carefully negotiated. Traffic lights were not strictly observed and the lines in the centre of the street needed painting. Small yellow taxis darted between older cars, hooting loudly and driving at speed through puddles or dust, spraying pedestrians walking close to the kerb. Every time a tram made its way down the street, the overhead cables spat like firecrackers adding to the ruckus. All the vehicles emitted potent fumes contributing to the pollution. I used to wait for a mother and child before crossing the street; I knew they would take less risk than younger men who weaved in and out between speeding traffic.

Despite the poverty and despair, the standard of education was astonishingly high. The Arts were an integral part of the lifestyle and most children played a musical instrument. When I mentioned Shakespeare, I was impressed that they knew so much about his work. I later learnt that the entire works of Shakespeare had been translated into Armenian and his plays were performed regularly.

Three times a week I took Armenian lessons with the help of a young professor who came to my hotel. He taught me the alphabet of this Indo-European language, how to write it, and basic conversation. I had little idea how useful it would be until one afternoon I was invited to visit the local television station. Most television programs were relayed in Russian from Moscow but the local station produced some Armenian programs, albeit under the watchful eye of Soviet authorities.

During my visit it was lightheartedly suggested that I take a screen test. Only afterwards, when someone announced I should front a weekly English language program, did I realise what I had let myself in for. Later, I preferred to remember it as a new door opening rather than an unnerving challenge. A director produced some filmed extracts of day-to-day scenarios such as shopping, visiting the doctor, going to the airport etc. My task was to write short scripts to illustrate the scenes and then present them in Armenian and English.

My Armenian professor was commandeered to help. I wrote the scripts in English, he translated them into Armenian and together we rehearsed my speaking them in both languages. The recording studio contained a small wooden dais, a single wooden chair and a tiny table. Bottled water was non-existent and I was warned to sip the small glass of water I was given because there might not be any more. Recording under lights is thirsty work so at times this proved taxing. My director learnt his first word of English and used it to chilling effect. When it was my cue to begin and a red light flashed before me, he called through from the adjoining room: "Smile, Julia, SMILE!"

I tried to learn each script by heart but kept a copy on the table in case my mind went a blank. Whenever there was a prolonged power cut, we packed up and left. My producer would arrange a time next day to finish the program and warned me to return wearing the same outfit and to have my hair and make-up as before. The two parts of the recorded program would then be spliced together.

When the first programme was broadcast, it was well received and many more followed. Before I knew it I was asked to head another series, this time all in English, talking about famous names and places in the West. When I returned to London on short breaks, I collected suitable slides and information on, say, Sir Winston Churchill, Shakespeare's birthplace, or the homes and lives of American presidents. I wrote scripts about these new subjects and presented them. Sir Winston Churchill was particularly admired in Armenia, not least because he was known to have been partial to a spot of locally made Armenian brandy.

I was based in Armenia for almost two years. The Cold War ended in 1991, soon after I left, and the country then underwent rapid change. Armenians in the diaspora contributed to the resurgence of their newly independent homeland and the local economy gained momentum.

I have returned several times and each time marvelled at the progress. I reflect with deep affection on the time I spent among a nation appallingly afflicted yet determined to recover from an unmitigated tragedy. Today, the places I once knew are barely recognisable. The earthquake-ravaged city of Leninakan has been renamed and new apartment buildings, solidly built and no more than four storeys high, have replaced the ramshackle huts. There are broad highways and Western-style hotels. Yerevan is a modern metropolis with European boutiques, supermarkets, souvenir shops and grand hotels. Hotel Armenia has been refurbished to a high standard. The statue of Lenin is long gone and lining the streets are flower stalls and coffee shops with outdoor terraces and coloured awnings. Traffic flows freely and traffic lights are obeyed.

International airlines have opened the way to easier access and tourism is accelerating. Every time I revisit this small Christian country of three million, I look at older ladies and recall the hardship they endured trying to raise children and finding food for the table. I remember the hospitality when I was invited into their homes and how once they made me a birthday cake three times the normal size. Their kindness remains but although many are still poor, in place of chaos and despair, today there is hope and boundless energy.

Life as a Global Volunteer

Meeting the class in Romania – horrors of an orphanage
– poverty and pollution in Ukraine – a medical calamity
– against the elements in Mongolia – summer festival –
places I could not go

Before entering the room, I had expected a class of seven or eight. Instead, there sat twenty-three, a sea of young curious faces, and the boldest launching a barrage of questions. "How old are you?" "Are you married?" "How many pets do you have?"

The head of the English Department introduced me to this class of children, aged between eleven and fourteen, and then left the room. An interpreter remained and she sat on a chair in a corner the other side of the blackboard. It turned out that her talents were rarely needed; if a child could not make themselves understood, those around them soon helped.

In 2001, at Barlad's Gheorghe Rosa Codreanu National College, five hours' drive northeast of Bucharest, Romania, these children had volunteered to attend school during their holidays. I knew that I had to maintain their enthusiasm; failure to do so would mean a morale-crushing dropout rate. Fortunately, they were eager to learn and not shy. Once the initiation was over, they settled down. Over the next two weeks, as long as I prepared my daily 9am to 1pm teaching sessions, their interest remained steadfast. Sometimes their enthusiasm was overwhelming. When I suggested they take a break, not least because I needed one myself, only half the class left the room. The more astute grabbed the opportunity for one-on-one conversation with their teacher.

During the years that I worked overseas as a global volunteer, few of the people I met, young or old, matched the exuberance of the Romanian children. It seemed nothing could keep them down and they were as anxious to look after me as I was to watch over them. Within days I knew a lot about their lives and priorities. When I asked them to write down five items they would take if they were abandoned on a desert island, I expected these to include computers, clothes and sports equipment. But no, to a child, they modified 'items' to include family members and pets. One student did list his entire wardrobe, announcing with great aplomb: "I carry it on my back. ONE item!" In general, though, material assets were of low priority. Few of them owned a Walkman (then all the rage in the West) and nobody had their own computer. Only two brought a writing utensil to class and, at most, three or four wore a watch. Some told me proudly that they went to the local Internet café and had their own email addresses.

A few days later I set another exercise, asking them what they would buy if they had US$1 million to spend. The money could not be invested or saved. Now, I thought, they *had* to choose material items. But what did they pick? Many chose cars for their parents; round-the-world airline tickets for themselves; and, without a second thought, allocated a large part of the $1 million to aid the poor in their country.

It was a sobering moment. Children so young and with few of the advantages kids in the UK or the USA take for granted, yet thinking so much about others. Many wanted to travel, but knew the opportunities were small. With an average wage of £60 a month, most of their parents could not even afford a secondhand car.

During my final week, and anxious to hold their attention, I introduced more unorthodox lessons with outdoor walks, and treated them all to lunch at a local pizza parlour. In the restaurant they whistled at the grand total and insisted on checking the bill while I marvelled at the low price.

I became a global volunteer in large part due to my love of travel and wishing to visit countries less well known and off the beaten tourist track. Having already lived and worked in Armenia, I was prepared for challenging living conditions and looked forward to meeting people who, for the most part, could not afford to travel themselves. Then based in Florida, it also made sense for me to escape the overwhelmingly hot and humid summers there, and to sign up for short periods of work in undeveloped places.

Global Volunteers, the company I volunteered with over several years, was and remains a non-profit, nonsectarian international development organisation based in St. Paul, Minnesota. At the time I worked for them, the organisation coordinated more than 150 teams of volunteers each year, serving in many countries with work projects such as teaching English, child care, building schools and community centres, repairing homes, assisting in natural resource projects and business instruction. The volunteers stayed several weeks and paid their own fares along with a supplement to the host organisation which provided accommodation and board.

As I soon discovered, the work experience was not so much about how much could be accomplished but rather interaction and better understanding between people of diverse cultures.

Not all the work in Romania was as inspiring as that in the G.R.C. National College. While I was there, a second team had undertaken to work in a local orphanage where conditions were deprived and depressing. Here babies and young children were handed in not because they were unloved but because their parents simply could not afford to keep them. Some parents returned to visit their children but many were permanently abandoned.

Although I was officially teaching English, I took a taxi one afternoon and joined some of the volunteers working in the orphans' wing at the local hospital. There the children lived in appalling, cramped conditions with no outdoor play area, no solid food and shared clothes. The volunteers arrived to find babies and toddlers in cloth nappies with accompanying rashes. The team bought up large stocks of disposable nappies wherever they could find them, and each morning the remains of our hotel breakfast was scooped up and taken for the children.

The first toddlers I saw sat on the floor of a tiny playroom banging their heads against a wall. Some stared at me suspiciously, others hopefully. Two scrambled over and put their arms around my neck, wanting to be hugged. Others, wary of strangers and fleeting affection, remained detached. Thirty babies and toddlers were crammed into a few dismal rooms. Many had special needs. One four-year-old never spoke and another refused to wear clothes. Each time this little boy was dressed, he tried to tear everything off. Because of their poor diet, the children were generally undersized.

Local nursing aides – and there were too few – struggled to provide care. The volunteers worked beside them, changing nappies, holding and rocking those children who wanted to be held, or playing with others. Each afternoon there was a scurry to find matching shoes so the children could go outside. The youngest were lifted into pushchairs and wheeled a short distance down a dilapidated trail to the fence by the hospital entrance. With noses pressed against the wire, they stared at passing traffic or cows in a distant field. This was their only access to the world beyond the hospital. Punctually at 4pm, they were taken back to their rooms. Each so-called bedroom had six to eight cots, lined end to end along two walls. Before the door was locked, the children would begin wailing, aware they were being shut away until next morning.

In Ukraine, I served twice on a team that was visiting Zaporizhzhya in the southeast of the country. A dispiriting place but with kind and generous local people, all struggling to overcome hardship and anxious to learn about the West. As always I took with me my volunteers' manual and a resource guide for teaching English. In addition I had teaching aids including a pack of cards, coloured chalk, felt-tip pens, maps, family photographs and at least one American fashion magazine. The magazine, used as a reward for good attention, proved indispensable and was not only read by girls. Young Ukrainians had a deep yearning to learn about life in the United States. When I passed round Post-It notes to a group of teenage students and asked each of them to write down what they would like to ask me, there was a scramble to comply and my interpreter, also called Julia, went from one group to the next. If they could not manage to write in English,

I told them to write in Ukrainian or Russian, and Julia would relay the contents. When the notes were gathered, several of the questions were similar. "Is America as we see it on television?" they asked. Naturally I then asked what had they had been watching to which there came the immediate chorus of: "Melrose Place!"

In the '90s, Melrose Place was a long-running American soap opera centring around a group of young adults living in an apartment complex in West Hollywood. The series had great appeal as entertainment but never portrayed an accurate picture of how most Americans lived. For the Ukrainian students, however, it formed the basis of their perception of the United States. When I pointed out some of the realities, they listened intently. They had no idea, for instance, that pollution was as prevalent in Los Angeles as it was in many of their cities.

During my second visit to the area, I spoke to a group of university students who were about to graduate as engineers. Most of them spoke little English so through an interpreter I asked what type of work they would be looking for. To my surprise, they hung their heads in shame. One eventually muttered something about how he just wanted to get a job, anything, perhaps drive a taxi. In this country where living standards were so low and unemployment so high, these bright young people had mentally acclimatised to the fact that they had to accept any type of work. Any ambition they might have had was quashed by reality.

It was on my second visit that one of our team of volunteers slipped on an unmarked step leading into a bathroom and broke her hip. I went with her in an antiquated ambulance to the local hospital. It must have been an agonising ride for her as the old roads were heavily potholed. Even worse, when we arrived, construction work was taking place in the entrance hall of the hospital and dust was flying. I sat with her for several hours amid the noise and disruption until she was eventually taken to the X-ray Department. Later she was admitted overnight into a dirty room with soiled linen and dark damp patches on the walls. Next day she was flown by Medivac out of the country for surgery in Germany and eventually made a good recovery. Had she been a local resident and fallen, she would have been forced to stay in bed, to heal or not, and might have remained wheelchair-bound for the rest of her life. At that time in Ukraine, there was no surgery for hip replacements.

It is a sad fact of life that in poor countries the poorest, weakest and youngest sink rapidly. With restricted opportunities and high unemployment, many have no way to progress and they give up hope. They fall victim to alcoholism, homelessness, disease and burn-out. Poor infrastructure, sanitation, climate and politics add to the dilemma. When food or water or both are hard to come by, life is a daily struggle just to survive. Of course this can happen to the poor in rich countries too, but they invariably have better support systems.

On the Greek island of Crete, living conditions for local people and our volunteer team were better. Although the children tended to be mischievous, at times verging on dangerous, the beauty of the surroundings offset the trauma the team had in controlling a bunch of young hooligans. As with all my service programmes, I learnt to do something new and well out of my comfort zone. There one evening, taking a walk with the team in the hills, a local shepherd gave me instructions on how best to milk a goat. If you haven't tried it, it is not as easy as it looks. If the goat actually acquiesces to being milked by a stranger, one has to pull very hard to succeed!

A few years after serving with *Global Volunteers,* I headed out on my own under the auspices of another organisation, *People To People International,* this time to Mongolia. PTPI has its headquarters in Kansas City, Missouri, and a presence with global chapters in 125 countries. Established by President Dwight D. Eisenhower in 1956, its mission was and remains to enhance international understanding and friendship through educational, cultural and humanitarian activities.

Travelling to Mongolia from Florida was a seemingly endless journey. I had five flights from West Palm Beach, changing planes in Dallas, Los Angeles, Seoul and Beijing. Due to the cancellation of the final flight to Ulaan Baatar, the Mongolian capital, and a subsequent two-day layover in Beijing, the outbound journey took almost five days. Fortunately I met three other Western travellers also detained in Beijing, and together we hailed a taxi and visited an enormous Chinese market, one outing I would never have undertaken alone.

Working in Mongolia presented unique problems, this country having arguably the worst climate in the world. Sandwiched between Russia and China, the Gobi Desert to the south dominates a third of the country while Siberia looms beyond its northern border. I timed my arrival for mid-May in order to miss the long sub-arctic winter. Even so, I needed a thick wool coat against the spring chill. What I was less prepared for, during the first few weeks, were the fierce dust storms that whipped up with little warning. At the first onset, I would run scurrying for cover, trying to protect my eyes from swirling particles. If this wasn't trying enough, once the dust storms abated, the rains came. Torrential storms made the poor roads temporarily impassable; water and dust combined into quagmires of mud, leaving stranded pedestrians wondering whether to zigzag around the mess or attempt to leap over it. On the other side, speeding vehicles, particularly the ubiquitous yellow taxis that whizzed around the capital, forged through the mire, spraying anyone within range from head to toe.

Summer suddenly arrived in June with day temperatures soaring into the eighties (Fahrenheit) before plummeting again each night. The only advantage as far as these changes in climate were concerned was the overall lack of humidity.

Employees at the bank in Ulaan Baatar, where I taught English, were eager students. Although Mongolian was their native language, many spoke Russian and a few spoke passable Chinese (Mandarin) or Korean. To be in my class, they had to have taken English for at least one year in school. Without an interpreter, I relied on those who were more proficient to help those who knew less.

I had been provided with a small apartment only a few minutes' walk from the bank's main office. This temporary home was rudimentary in terms of furniture and utilities. The curtains were old, the place badly needed painting and my morning showers were usually cold. However, I was grateful to have my own place to stay and very happy to have my own toilet.

Mongolia is one of many countries I've been to where sanitary conditions left much to be desired. Cleanliness is not next to godliness in poor countries, it can't be. You simply do your best. And if you're careful, you'll probably be fine. I took two short courses of antibiotics with me but fortunately never needed them. I did drink bottled water but I was assured tap water was fine. Unfortunately poor hygiene leads to a high risk of infection, and in the outer reaches of this country there were still occasional outbreaks of bubonic plague.

Among those who suffered most were children and not only from disease. In the capital I saw some young people, abandoned by their parents, left to sleep under city buildings. In winter, temperatures dropped to -40C yet many of them were forced to live huddled together among the pipes beneath buildings where it was marginally warmer. If not for the caring auspices of several overseas Christian organisations, who knows how many would have perished.

I lived and worked in Ulaan Bataar for almost two months. During the week, I ate lunch in the bank's canteen. Mongolians are avid meat eaters and the two courses for employees both included meat, either beef or mutton. This was accompanied by sticky white rice or mashed potato, and occasionally some chopped tomatoes, onions or cabbage. Fish was never served. The only time I saw a fish was in the frozen foods' section of a large local supermarket. There was a label in English on the side of this strange specimen saying simply '*Fish*', presumably to tempt foreigners seeking a change of diet.

With time to spare at weekends, I had a silk dress made-to-measure and went shopping for locally made cashmere scarves. There were also unforgettable performances by the State Academic Opera and the Ballet Theatre. I once heard a riveting performance of *La Traviata* and an interesting if less memorable one of *Carmen* sung in Mongolian. Unforgettable, for another reason was an anniversary dinner at the bank where I worked. The entertainment consisted of different singers, some in traditional costume, entertaining guests followed by a firework display *inside* the hotel ballroom. Fireworks and sparklers shot up from some point beneath the podium lights!

I spent another weekend in the country, a guest of the bank's CEO, trying archery and riding a strange-looking yak with twisted horns and a long matted coat.

The bank employees were exceptionally kind. No matter how harsh the conditions under which they lived, they were constantly looking out for me. On my second day, a new computer was installed in the bank's Board Room for my exclusive use. Without asking, they knew I would want to communicate with family and friends (this was before the era of mobile phones).

Of Mongolia's 2.6 million population, more than a third lived in the capital. This left vast tracts of sparsely populated country with spectacular landscapes and not a telephone pole in sight. Mountain ranges, forests, steppes, and deserts were all part of the rugged and unspoiled land, free of fences and home to thousands of friendly nomads. My guidebook called it a Boy Scout's dream and certainly it was a paradise for those who love to camp, wash in rivers and repair broken jeeps. There were plenty of young backpackers in Ulaan Baatar, preparing to head into the outback or having just returned from it. Even more intrepid were those adventurers who visit in winter and head north or west to skate on the lakes, fish through deep ice or study the reindeer. I asked one young Swede, who was passionate about the winter experience, how she managed the sub-zero temperatures. "Of course you have to be appropriately dressed," she conceded. "But as you skate, you can watch fish swimming under the ice!" Later I learnt that temperatures in the Gobi desert way to the south can also fall far below freezing.

Mongolians who lived in the country clung to a mostly nomadic lifestyle, tending herds of sheep and goats. They lived in traditional *'gers'*, which are large, round tents made out of felt and canvas, with brightly coloured doors and an opening at the top. Supported by a collapsible wooden frame, these hardy little structures can withstand almost anything the climate throws at them.

Within the *ger*, the stove sits in the centre and the smoke exits at the top. Beds are always positioned on either side of the door; saddles and other riding gear are stored to the left of the entrance, and honoured guests and elders have a special seat at the rear of the home. There are rules of etiquette for visitors but foreigners are forgiven for lapses, such as sitting on the wrong side (it's men to the left and women to the right) or whistling or taking food with the left hand.

Living in a *ger* means sacrificing many creature comforts we take for granted. Nevertheless, some nomads have entered the 21st century by taking on solar power and satellite dishes. The toilet situation remains outdated; it's do-as-you-must-where-you-will but well away from the home.

Some Mongolian nomads owned trucks. When it came to dismantling their homes and moving on, they simply disassembled them and loaded them into the rear of the vehicle. Others who lacked the convenience had to load everything on top of camels or yaks. With nomads moving as often as four times a year, according to season and better grazing pasture for their herds of sheep, goats and cattle, it was and remains an arduous life.

Clearly, in order to survive, it's imperative one has some sort of pick-me-up when the going gets tough. Herders have the very thing to offset the darkest moments, in the form of a devilish homemade brew called *airag*. This milky concoction has a sour taste and noticeable alcoholic content. More off-putting still is the fact that it's made from fermented mare's milk. In place of *airag* there was also plenty of vodka. One particular local brand, Chinggis Khaan, had a picture of the national hero on every bottle and was available in most stores.

I resorted to vodka and orange juice at weekends. After some serious street trudging, I located an ice tray in the State Department store in the centre of the city. The tray was vivid green and included eight little receptacles all in the shape of hearts. Clearly made for children and ice lollies, it was not ideal but suited my purpose.

In the country there were more horses than people. Mongolians are phenomenal horsemen, and horses live everywhere except Ulaan Baatar, although they appear for important parades on national holidays. What the Mongolian horse lacks in stature, it makes up for in vigour. It may be small but visitors are well-advised not to call it a pony. They are also strictly work animals and treated as such. When I ventured close to one group, my city companions warned me away with the deterrent they could also be mean.

Every July, a national three-day festival incorporates the local sports of horse riding, archery and wrestling. It is the biggest event of the year for both Mongolians and tourists, and takes place in and around the capital. The Naadam (meaning holiday) Festival kicks off with army parades and musical fanfares outside the State Parliament House fronting Sukhbaatar Square in the centre of Ulaan Baatar. After this, everyone heads to the main stadium for opening ceremonies, which include athletes, more marching bands and local theatrical interlopers.

There's some pageantry and the thrill of seeing Chinggis Khaan (Genghis Khan), Mongolia's greatest warrior, reincarnated to lead his men in 12th or 13th century battle attire at full gallop round the stadium.

The horse races involve children aged 5-13 who race over open countryside for up to eighteen miles. There are six categories, all dependent upon the age of the horse rather than the rider. Before the event, the horses are fed a special diet and carefully trained. Given the difficult terrain, each race is an endurance test for rider and horse, and demands skill and courage.

The archery contests are for adults who wear the traditional dress known as a *del*. This heavy silk coat (worn by men and women) falls to mid-calf with a sash and hat. When I was there, younger Mongolians rarely wore the *del*, preferring snug-fitting Western-style outfits and, for the city slickers, high heels.

The final sport of wrestling saw contestants looking considerably less modest in short, tight pants with matching tight vests in red or blue. This unflattering ensemble was completed with a pair of thick, heavy boots.

The first day of the Naadam Festival was undoubtedly the most important. The second saw fewer contestants and the third was pretty much null and void. One spectator informed me that the final day was used by many to sleep off what was imbibed over the course of the first two.

* * *

There were countries for which, despite tragedy and disaster, volunteers were either carefully selected, or entire teams prevented from serving. One of these countries was Haiti. I volunteered to work there following the earthquake in January, 2010 but was told it could be dangerous for a woman of my age and race.

The same occurred in 2004, two years after a devastating tsunami hit Sri Lanka. This time I made a private visit, taking a tour of the island and the damaged coastline. The US Government had determined that due to ongoing unrest associated with the Tamil Tigers in the north of the island, it could not guarantee the safety of volunteers. With my air ticket already purchased, I went alone and wrote up the experience for a local paper in Florida.

Colombo, the capital, had been unaffected by the tsunami and remained a thriving metropolis with all the accompanying congestion and occasional chaos of most major cities. Cars and *tuktuks* (small motorised three-wheeled rickshaws) competed with old bicycles and dilapidated buses along the dusty roads. Fish sellers buzzed along on motorbikes with a pair of scales dangling precariously to one side, and large fish tanks slopping water behind the driver's seat.

Along the coast, new homes were being built, supposedly set back from the beach, but some of them still seemed perilously close to the shore. Despite the tsunami and its toll on people and homes, Sri Lanka had to be one of the most beautiful places I have seen. In the centre of the island were high rural areas with endless tea plantations stretching along vast slopes, thriving amid the wet terrain and cooler climate. A few farmers were still using water buffalo to pull their carts and the animal's milk was made into curd. "Very good for the digestion," my driver told me. "Very delicious with honey."

I took him at his word but never tried any; the breakfast buffet in the hotels where I stayed disdained such traditional fare. What I missed in the morning, however, I made up for at night. The local drink, known as *arrack,* is a strong alcoholic brew drawn from coconut flowers. Lithe young men known as 'toddy tappers' climbed the coconut trees and tapped the flowers for juice which in turn was sold to the local distillery. The liquor had the combined flavour of whisky and brandy. It made a longer and, for me, a more palatable drink when served as a cocktail and blended with passion fruit.

I was told that the elephants, a stunning feature of the island, both wild and domesticated, had sensed the impending tsunami and in the national park they were seen to have retreated to higher ground. Certainly they were highly regarded and respected by local people. On entering Yala National Park, every visitor is handed a cleansing towel and a board that says: "You have just entered a wildlife reservation/sanctuary. Please treat it as such. No honking or tooting or blowing your own trumpet unless you are an elephant."

At Home...

During the course of my life and living in several countries, I have had a number of residences, ranging from a downtrodden hotel suite through to London flats and upscale Florida apartments. In my late teens and early twenties, I was a renter in London sharing with others in a home or flat, and once alone in a bedsit for a month. At this time, parents frowned on young unmarried couples living together so young women tended to cohabit in threes, fours or even fives in shared accommodation. During these heady years of youth, there was fun in groups and we shared not only utility bills and rent, but our personal friends and household chores.

In 1980 I bought my first home, a small flat off Kensington Church Street, which at the time was bursting with antique stores save for the southernmost part where there were a few trendy boutiques including Biba. As years went by, some of the antique stores and Biba disappeared, and today the lower end of the street has become a Mecca for skin rejuvenation, nail salons and coffee shops.

The first builder who ventured into my flat was a fit young rugby playing Irishman. According to my lease, it was mandatory to have carpet to limit the transmission of noise between floors and I chose an impractical cream covering to make the place look light and bright. Today I have friends, primarily from other parts of Europe, who disapprove of wall-to-wall carpeting, dismissing it as an unhygienic bug-infested aberration. Admittedly a carpet has drawbacks and needs regular cleaning, but it does afford a certain cosiness through long winter months.

As for the Irishman, he was young and lithe with a lilt to match. My newly fitted carpet with a deep pile meant the doors would not easily close and needed shaving down. He sized up the work, quoted lower than the two previous estimates I'd received, and sealed the deal. Later the same week, the affected doors were removed from their hinges and the work discharged in the middle of the exterior corridor. In bygone days, rules and regulations relating to the building were on the lenient side, and nobody interfered or tried to stop him. When done, said Irishman suggested he return one evening with a takeaway and a bottle or two to imbibe. There followed the celebration of the perfect closing of my flat doors and the opening of another more personal one.

I have now owned this little flat for over forty years. In that time it has been refurbished more than once but usually in stages. During the first refit, floor to ceiling mirrors were erected in every room save the kitchen to visually enlarge the area, and fitted cupboards were installed to better utilise the limited space. Over the years the bathroom has been remodelled twice, the first time including the removal of some gruesome green tiles and the advent of peach units including a corner bath. As trends changed, after fifteen years the peach and accompanying gold fittings looked passé and I placed myself in the hands of a new company. I threw out the bath and, mindful of advancing years, ordered a shower, complete with non-slip surface and a seat, as yet unused.

With a flat so small, it has always been imperative that I vacate the premises to give the builders free rein. Confidence is the operative word, so during the latest bathroom renovation I flew off to visit friends in Florida. Neighbours were incredulous that I would go so far away while work was in progress but my main concern was whether or not the room would be functional by the time I returned. In the event, there was one harrowing moment when, as I boarded my return flight, the builders emailed photos of my gutted bathroom. Fortunately, the pictures had been taken a week before and by the time I entered my front door, the remodelled room was almost, but not quite, finished. Over the next two days as finishing touches were applied, I used the *rest* room (lovely American term that, so much more genteel than *toilet*) in my local Marks & Spencer.

Let's face it, bathrooms are the worst room in the home to remodel. So much work in a comparatively small space. I had no less a problem when I lived in Florida, only there a kind neighbour gave me the use of her spare bathroom while mine was revamped. Unfortunately, this time the protracted length of the procedure had tempers fraying on both sides.

In Palm Beach, I owned a one-bed, one-bath apartment with an exterior terrace. I might never have undertaken any refurbishment had a hurricane not hit close to Miami one summer and caused destruction to homes and landscape. The subsequent effect alerted State authorities and insurance companies, both of which determined new regulations for homeowners. Obliged to meet stricter standards, I chose to enclose my terrace before exterior hurricane shutters were erected. With the upheaval came the hope, later realised, that the value of my apartment would increase with a larger living area.

Being a novice at renovation in America, and also because I worked in my home, I was loath to undertake the remodelling of more than one room per year. Once begun, however, I was inspired to continue, enduring what I later termed 'reconstructive surgery' over three years. Now you might think that I would become accustomed to the annual upheaval but this never happened because each year, once it was over, I blocked out the noise and disruption and basked in the glow of achievement.

I selected a builder from a shortlist recommended by the condominium management. As it happened, the person I chose was not simply a contractor but an ace developer who for much of his time built large swathes of homes some miles inland. As head of his company, he breezed in one Saturday, took one look round my ramshackle place, was politely silent a moment, then determined to take me under his wing and help. In hindsight, enclosing the terrace and inserting new windows proved to be relatively minor. The effect, however, was dramatic, and friends readily acknowledged the enlarged living area was a definite upgrade.

The second year, I remodelled the kitchen. This time I took my microwave and retreated to eat, sleep and work in my bedroom. A new refrigerator, delivered early, was temporarily housed in my living room and was useful for mealtimes as well as other more desperate moments when the stress or mess proved overwhelming. As weeks passed, my contractor felt sorry about the number of frozen dinners I was consuming and invited me out for pasta at a local restaurant. When I gobbled up the linguine indecently fast, he surreptitiously tipped the remains from his plate onto mine. It was obvious he was afraid I might do an Oliver Twist and ask for more.

Once again, my remodelled room was a striking improvement and in the euphoria of accomplishment, I set aside the associated disorder and anguish.

The third and final year saw the bathroom demolished and refitted, and this was the killer. My contractor promptly assigned me someone I later lightheartedly referred to as my psychiatrist but who in reality was an interior designer. When I protested I didn't need such a professional, I was warned sternly of the pecuniary consequences of making wrong decisions regarding fixtures and fittings.

I have to say that Joel, my appointed shrink, was more honest than anyone in preparing me for the ordeal ahead. He cautioned me that the operation was likely to take longer than I had been led to believe and boosted my morale when it flagged. He begged me to hang in over a long weekend when I was getting desperate and painstakingly assured me that the vanity unit he had designed was not going to look like the monstrous carbuncle the frame suggested it might. Hard as he tried, however, I verged close to a nervous breakdown. The gutting of the old bathroom went without incident, but the remodelling brought more than a hiccup or two. I woke one Monday morning after a weekend spent ruminating on the delays, and assailed my contractor as to why work was not proceeding faster. "Where does the buck stop?" I demanded shrilly and more than once. "Weeks have passed and I'm in limbo! What's happening? You told me...you *assured* me...". Blah-blah. Seriously agitated, I was on a roll.

He remained uncharacteristically calm, which led me to the sneaking suspicion that he was accustomed to clients' protests. In a tone possibly reserved for ladies he considers unbalanced, he moaned slowly: "I hear you, Julia. I hear you."

But my outburst produced the desired effect. In retrospect I can see that a normally calm lady, when suddenly flustered, can achieve a lot more than someone given to regular bouts of irritation. A flurry of activity ensued, my phone ringing almost off the hook to schedule appointments for plumbing and fittings. Within days the finishing touches were applied.

The morning after my outburst, my contractor called back and asked impishly if I was in a better mood. Well, yes, I laughed. Builders, I accept, are a breed unto themselves. A week or so later, he came round to inspect the new room. As I wrote out a cheque, he inquired sweetly which part of my home I would next like to remodel. Taken aback, but smiling brightly, I muttered something about having little left to redo. What I could *not* bring myself to say was that while flush with the excitement of my new bathroom, did he not realise that I needed a little more time to forget?

* * *

I can think back to all the homes I have lived in and be thankful. Most of them have offered comfort and security. However, it only takes a well-publicised local jewellery heist to remind me that, besides the sentimental loss of personal possessions in a robbery, there invariably lies a good deal of unpleasantness and anxiety. One has only to be a victim of a home robbery once to have an inkling what that might be. There may be some thieves who go in and out, grab what they want, and leave with little trace or disruption. Unfortunately, in three generations of my family that has not been the case.

My maternal grandmother lived in a lovely home in Pinner, Middlesex. She lived with her maid, Annie, who looked after her for many years long after my grandfather died. He had survived fighting in the First World War and founded an insurance company but then succumbed to cancer at what we would today consider a relatively young age. My grandmother soldiered on with local visits from friends and family, including her three children and a host of grandchildren. Annie prepared tea for these occasions, and became famous for making cucumber sandwiches look like a work of art.

One day a professional team of crooks set out to off-load my grandmother of some of her possessions. They sent a stake-out party to her house, posing as sellers of locally made lace and linen, but she was smart enough to notice the foreign tags and sent them packing. Unfortunately, gaining admittance was sufficient for the thieves to look round her home, check entrances and exits, and choice items. They returned in the dead of night and set about removing what they wanted.

During their work, they had the gall to sit at her kitchen table, open her refrigerator and have a snack. Once replete, they left used plates on the table and departed by the window through which they had entered, carefully setting sacks over the ground outside to cover their footprints. They took off and neither they nor their booty, primarily solid silverware, were heard or seen again. Thankfully, my grandmother and Annie slept uninterrupted through the night.

Just over a year after my father died, my mother moved into a smaller house in a village a few miles away. She took with her personal possessions and some of the furniture and left our original home on the market still unsold. Despite the house being almost empty, thieves, or more likely young hooligans, broke in and took a look round. Either out of spite because there was little to be gleaned, or from nervous excitement, they relieved themselves in various parts of our former home.

They snapped up a few pewter mugs but otherwise made off with very little. Before leaving, presumably as a final mark of contempt, they went into an upstairs bathroom, plugged the tub, and turned on the taps. Mercifully they chose the bath over the front porch which meant the water ran down and out of the house rather than saturating the entire lower floor.

Years later it was my turn. I was away when one very slim thief broke through a small rubbish locker and wriggled his or her way into my tiny London flat. In an attempt to locate a key for the front door and thereby escape with large items, the thief ransacked the place. Fortunately no spare key was found so the plunderer had to make do with a video and a few pocket-size items before wriggling back through the bottom of the locker and out undetected.

The police were very polite; the fingerprint expert was so meticulous that it took me days to get rid of the special filmy dust applied to the telephone (which had been moved and possibly used) and all around my toilet. After my mother's experience I told myself I was lucky the thief had used the toilet. For me the worst part of the ordeal was the first night back in my newly violated home. No matter how high I live, I have always been wary of intruders and darkness, and that first evening before going to bed, I must have checked each cupboard several times over, twice ensured the windows were shut, and even looked in the bath tub just to reassure myself nobody was there.

God forbid I had encountered anyone because I would surely have died of terror without uttering a word.

One friend was sensitive enough to call and ask how I felt. That call meant a lot because at least I could talk about it. However, the truth is that no matter how much we have, or how little we lose, the violation is much more than a loss of personal possessions. It is a frightening invasion of privacy and a shattering destroyer of trust. On a more positive note, my rubbish locker has been sealed for years; the building now has CCTV all over the place and the present staff are wonderfully diligent.

* * *

Spring cleaning, done well, is an odious task. To accomplish it to an acceptable level entails more than cleaning, it demands clearing out. Of course if we never get around to more than a perfunctory spit and polish throughout the year, then this traditionally industrious time presents a nightmare.

To some people, spring cleaning is anathema. Hoarders probably don't even consider its existence because they could never surmount their possessions to reach, let alone clean, the top of a curtain rail. And as for clearing out, their protests would extend to 'I might need it' or 'It's part of my past.'

Not everyone likes having a cleaning lady. Those who work at home dread her arrival because it means they must either endure the sound of machines and other noise associated with her work, or vacate the premises until she is through. If they can abide neither, then like me they do the job themselves. Unfortunately the latter can lead to indifferent regard towards order and cleanliness. Standards tend to drop with hasty or irregular appraisal. I once knew an elderly academic who derailed criticism by nipping it in the bud. When she perceived raised eyebrows at the state of chaos in her home, she drew herself up with eccentric grandeur and announced with aplomb: "I am above dust."

Most of us grit our teeth and do the best we can. Money can buy no escape from the seasonal assessment, evacuation and cleansing of goods and chattels. Not, that is, if it is done properly. There are, however, certain ways to make the process less vexing. The first of these is to prevent the work piling up all year. My advice would be to attack it in small doses and clear out a cupboard every other month. Attack the beast on a bad-weather day. Also, it's best to start out in the right frame of mind; an upbeat, ebullient, conquer-the-world sort of spirit is best. This way two hours of sorting one cupboard ensures a positive outcome and a feeling of satisfaction. Never try to do too much. Eight cupboards over a weekend could lead to serious depression and a therapist's couch. If you know you could not survive another session of spring cleaning under present circumstances, there is one last resort. The alternative is to move into a smaller home.

Small homes have few cupboards, shelves or furniture with drawers. Owners are forever discouraged from accumulating en masse because there is less place to store or display possessions. Areas to be cleaned and items to be dry-cleaned are reduced to the point you actually have time to look out of the window and enjoy the view.

For many of us books are a problem. Even with the Internet and downloading contents onto our I-Pads or Kindles, we still manage to accumulate the real hold-in-your-hand copies that are easier to read on the beach or to curl up with on the sofa. In London, when I had mirrors erected along one wall of my living room, I had first to remove bookshelves and several hundred books. Local charity shops benefited mightily and, to be truthful, I haven't missed the books or the dust they accumulate. I've also noticed that really ancient tomes can acquire a slightly musty smell that the very best housekeeper cannot erase. I have smelt it in stately homes, and while the odour cannot all be attributed to books they almost certainly contribute towards it. Also, how many of us re-read books we knew and loved years ago? We look at them, smile fondly, and pass on. And non fiction, particularly reference books, become outdated.

In the past, whenever I moved to live in another country, I bought a new large English dictionary and a thesaurus. For shorter stays I made do with pocket sized editions of the same. It followed that when I left a place, I donated both to a local school or library where they were always well received. These days computers halve the need for such books, although I still refer to them for explicit definitions or synonyms.

There's little doubt that people with large living areas and storage space tend to hoard more personal effects than those who live in small homes. Moreover, when space is unlimited, they have to withstand the temptation to reshuffle instead of discarding. Owners of gargantuan homes might tell you they had a monumental clearing out but the reality may be it was more of an evasive manoeuvring of possessions rather than an out-and-out purge of them.

Charity shops are a wonderful way of disposing of items we no longer need or want. I love to donate, to the extent that I jokingly tell friends that I play a large part in keeping such shops in business. There are plenty within walking distance of my flat, which makes me think they are not just doing well but thriving. And this belief is further enforced by signs in their windows earnestly entreating further donations.

Occasionally I wonder whether I overdid my ruthless disposal of items. I once took several framed prints that I decided I no longer wanted into my local charity shop. A few days later I saw one of them hanging on the wall beside the front window. I snuck in to see how much was on the price tag and was surprised to see the asking figure was almost £100. The following week the picture was gone, so I raced inside and asked what had happened to it. "They were all sold to a gentleman who, till he retired, worked for Prince Charles," came the reply. "He has a large collection all over his home. Hardly a space on the wall, I've seen them!"

I think my strictly limiting possessions is due in part to a lifetime of moving and travelling, which necessarily meant limiting how much I could take with me. Not one for involving international removal firms other than to convey small items such as paintings, I've always offloaded all but the most essential items, and in the United States sold homes fully furnished.

Having children leads to accumulation because of the memories and interests they engender. The hardest part must be for parents witnessing their offspring leaving the nest, but I've always felt that if children could be persuaded to take at least some of their past treasures with them when they go, it would lessen the load that one day has to be sorted.

At the moment my little flat is filled to capacity, mostly with clothes. I blame the pandemic because how can I offload something when I've had little opportunity to wear it? With restaurants and theatres closed so long, and family and friends kept apart, garments hang waiting to be worn. And some of them are new, obtained over the internet while I was twiddling my thumbs and wondering what would please me to have when I was denied so much else.

One day, when we have all well and truly recovered, I will sort and jettison again. After all, at the end of the day, it is only *stuff* which we cannot take with us...

Luca

Neighbourly conduct – Miss Frobisher – Jack-of-all-
Trades – CCTV and fire alarm – keeping a low profile

Originally, I considered a first person fictional
story around Luca (not his real name), creating a
beginning and an end while incorporating in the centre an
otherwise true narrative. The opening was to have seen
my character sitting in a solicitor's office and discovering
that upon Luca's demise he had, to my amazement,
bequeathed me his studio flat. It was in closing the tale,
ending it in a manner that respected Luca and his foibles,
that I eventually came to reconsider and opted not to
fictionalize our connection. So now I'm going to relate
the facts as accurately as I can and leave the denouement
to you.

Luca and I have owned flats in the same London
building for more than forty years. In all that time I have
known him only in passing and taken care not to become
involved or to engage him in lengthy conversation. The
truth is he makes me uncomfortable. If I were to grow
closer, I fear he might come knocking on my door,
intentionally obliging me to invite him inside, with
consequences that will readily become apparent.

I'm not sure whether Luca moved into the building
before I did but he was certainly living here as long as I
can remember. I was in my early thirties when I bought my

one-bedroom flat, and he was somewhat older although his precise age was always hard to gauge. In those early years I wrote in the mornings and then went out to part-time work from midday on. For some months I covered the lunch shift at the bar of a local pub, and for nearly two years I worked in reception for a team of architects. The work, while menial, was conveniently close to my flat and I could relax after writing, which I have always found mentally exhausting. More importantly, I needed the input of cash, however small, to keep me afloat.

Luca had a studio flat on a lower floor. Whenever we passed in the lobby or met in the launderette opposite the building, he was odiously polite. But that wasn't what made me uneasy, although it certainly did not endear him to me. You see, in those early days I was convinced he was a woman. I was so certain that when one of the porters referred to him as *Mr.* Romano, I corrected him. The porter was adamant and in the end I backed off, still sure I was right. At the time Luca was tall and slim, his facial features undeniably feminine and his voice soft and melodic. There was no doubting that he looked like a woman, while his eccentric way of dressing could have placed him on either side of the gender divide.

One evening, a few years after I moved in, I was having a drink with Miss Frobisher, an older neighbour who was always chatty and interested, a sure fire recipe for having her ear to the ground where other residents were concerned. She has long since sailed away but during those days I would occasionally invite her, and she enjoyed coming, to my flat for a drink. Sometimes I invited another neighbour and we had a mini cocktail party, an event that always thrilled Miss Frobisher, who dressed, albeit in a slightly outdated mode, for the occasion. One evening Luca's name came up. "He's a hermaphrodite," Miss Frobisher announced confidently. "And a hoarder." This was news to me. Until I confirmed the exact meaning of hermaphrodite I wasn't precisely sure what she was saying but, having done so, I experienced the mixed emotions of curiosity and compassion. Poor man. Or poor woman. How to live with attributes of both? Later I wondered what sort of proof she had to make such a statement and with such certainty. That Luca was outwardly different was never in doubt, but I had not considered he might have certain characteristics, or should I say organs, relating to both male and female. Come to think of it, how could Miss Frobisher, long retired as a physiotherapist, be so sure? Just how reliable was her knowledge of anatomy? I found it easier to accept that Luca was a hoarder, even though she admitted she had never seen the interior of his flat. And having a studio flat, just how much stuff he could accumulate was open to debate. I had heard that, among other jobs, he ran a stall on Portobello Road, which almost certainly meant he acquired bric-à-brac and sold it off. Indeed, I had seen him leaving early on a Saturday, trundling several wheelie-bags that appeared to be full, which might serve to confirm the rumour. If indeed he was heading to the market, then it made sense he might retain items he was unable to flog and over time overload his flat with those he was unable to sell.

The mystery surrounding Luca increased still further when I walked up the street one day and spotted him in a hairdressing salon, cutting a client's hair. What other qualifications, I wondered, did he possess or claim to have? A Jack-or-Jill-of-all-Trades came to mind, but that was no reason to judge him unkindly and anyway there are those who might say he possessed the entrepreneurial spirit and the more kudos to him.

Several things happened not long afterwards which made me think Miss Frobisher could be right in both matters but certainly the former. In my first years as a resident, I sometimes took the sun in late spring and summer up on the roof of my building. In those days this was permitted, today it is banned. The rooftop is not a particularly pleasant place and, having no protective railings at the sides, there's probably a security risk which an insurance company wouldn't condone. That's not to say I haven't recently been up there – rules can be bent, can't they? – but access has to be gained via the staff who hold keys to the padlock that opens the exit door. In order to acquire access today, one needs to be in good standing with the concierge (helped by a generous Christmas bonus). Today, Luca almost certainly would not qualify because he and the concierge do not get on, but more on that later. The exit door leads out onto a large expanse of what looks like tarmac but I'm not precisely sure of its make-up. It certainly doesn't bubble up under intense sun, but it is not very comfortable to lie on. I have always taken a mat plus a large towel.

One Saturday, I was up there basking on my back with my eyes half-closed, when the exit door opened and out stepped Luca. I sucked in my breath, closed my eyes and feigned to be asleep. Keeping a reasonable distance, Luca laid out his towel and we both lay in silence, widely spaced. An hour or so later, I heard him snoring. On hearing this, I slowly opened my eyes and turned to face him. He – and yes, from this point on, I accepted he was, outwardly anyway, predominantly male – was wearing a pair of baggy shorts. His chest bore no signs of breasts although it was definitely barrel-shaped, more rounded than I would have expected for a man. It was also hairless.

The second event, although it could hardly be called so, occurred one evening on my return from the London Budokwai. I had taken up judo to stay fit, and was returning from a practice session, carrying my kitbag and hurrying home for supper, when I met Luca in the lobby. I was also feeling the depressing onset of a sore throat and a slight thickening of mucus in my nose. I exchanged pleasantries with Luca and he made note of my nasal twang and thought I should take something to thwart the onset of a cold or worse. He had, he assured me, some medication to help and suggested I accompany him to his flat so he could find it. Anxious to escape, I assured him I was fine and had my own meds should I need any. Without wishing to be rude, but certainly ill-at-ease, I thanked him politely, then without waiting for the lift, raced up the four floors to my flat before he could follow. Next morning, down with an awful cold, Luca should have felt grateful that, if nothing else, he had escaped catching it. Of course it may have been that he had no ulterior motive and truly wanted to help, but it was a risk I was not willing to take.

The third and final incident concerned my going to the cinema with a neighbour (not Miss Frobisher, not the right genre for her) to see the film *Victor Victoria* with Julie Andrews. Julie played a woman who pretended to be a man in order to enhance her career. There is one particular scene in which she dresses as a man and performs in front of an audience. Slowly the camera pans round to show those in the audience, a cluster of strange people, their freakish appearance no doubt enhanced by make-up. That they were in a minority as far as sexual orientation was concerned was patently obvious, although today I admit the lines are more blurred. Among them, as you've probably guessed, sat Luca. I turned in my chair at the same moment my neighbour turned to me. We both recognised him. Weeks later, I saw Luca in the launderette and, against my better judgement, couldn't resist asking if he had been in the film. Somewhat coyly, but certainly pleased, he admitted he had been an extra.

My flat is indeed very small – but not as small as Luca's – and I love the location. For me it was first a perfect flat on boarding the real estate ladder, then a wonderful pied-a-terre when I was living overseas, and now it has morphed into a good place for retirement. I was alone when I bought the flat, and after a few years, another elderly resident (not Miss Frobisher or my cinema accomplice) determined to introduce me to a composer living on the floor below mine. We, that is the composer and I, subsequently married and moved to New York. He sold his flat, but I retained mine so that I could use it when returning to visit my mother who lived just north of London. For a while I allowed friends to use the flat when I was away, but after I had the bathroom remodelled I put word about that nobody could use it any more; I had too much cash invested in it. Also, my mother was elderly by then and I never knew when I might need to return at short notice. By deterring others it saved the awkwardness of asking them to leave and I was spared the discomfort of knowing they could not afford a local hotel for any length of time.

There is something else that might or might not be relevant. Because I do not know if Luca was responsible, he remains innocent until proven otherwise. I returned to London from Florida on one of my visits and discovered an anonymous letter waiting among a bundle of junk mail and bank statements. The postmark was illegible, my name misspelt and the childish handwriting elevated to the right at the end of each line. While the contents could be said to have been written by an admirer, parts of it were undoubtedly obscene. For openers, the author (surely too much of an accolade) was intent on thrashing me with sticks of rhubarb and celery and parading me naked down the high street. Later the fetish intent extended to intimate satisfaction including sexual fantasies of a bizarre nature. Setting aside the poor handwriting, the content of the letter was not badly written in that vocabulary and spelling were mostly correct.

Probably unwisely, I showed the letter to close friends. Nobody I knew had ever received such a missive so there was token oneupmanship. One of these friends thought I should hand it to the police, but I determined it was too late for that. Our fingerprints were all over both the letter and the envelope, and the latter probably included the paws of the postman. Besides, what could the police do? There was also the disquieting thought that I might be subjected to some probing questions and even ribald remarks, although perhaps that's unkind to officers who would (almost) certainly be professional. As far as I could tell, there were no telltale signs as to who had written it and thereby clues on which the police could work. The letter was mailed from a central post office but the rest of the postmark was illegible.

I kept the letter for many years then finally destroyed it. I was concerned that if it was read, possibly studied at length by my nieces and nephews after my demise, they might conjecture wrongly who had written it or what I might (or might not) have done to warrant receiving it. They would possibly conclude that their aunt had a darker side to her life of which they had hitherto been unaware. Anyway, the question of who wrote it will be forever unknown, although Luca remains on my list of suspects along with a judoka or two.

After I was divorced, I based myself in Florida. In all the years I was living overseas, I saw Luca only on my return visits. Then we politely acknowledged one another but little more. More often than not there was a short smile on my part and an exaggerated "Hel-LLO!" on his. I never saw him with other people; he was always alone. That he is a solitary soul is sad, but then nothing is ever what it seems and I was sure there was a side to him that I did not know.

So long away – almost thirty years – saw Luca and me age in the interim. Luca had filled out and adopted an even more bizarre appearance, favouring harem pants, caps with glitzy crystals dotted over the crown, and slip-on shoes that were sometimes mismatched. The porters – they too had changed over time – avoided him whenever possible. He featured on the shortlist of residents who were deemed problematic and, in Luca's case, unpredictable. There were times when he was morose and other times when he lied without compunction. He did not take kindly to ageing but this may have been partly on account of some health problems.

Maybe it was loneliness that also drove him to incorrigible habits. I sometimes thought that by not engaging with him I was being unkind, yet I couldn't help feeling anxious in his presence. I feared if I was kind or sympathetic in some way he might accost me in the lobby with any grievances he might have. And would a gentler stance on my part have moved him to a happier disposition towards staff and other residents? I doubted it. Reaching out to him might place me in peril, so I did nothing. Had I engaged in a closer relationship, while remaining on the periphery of friendship, I knew I would step out of my comfort zone.

Over time he owned an ever shorter fuse. He began lashing out with foul language to anyone who challenged him. Fortunately, our current concierge is someone who does not flinch when on the receiving end of Luca's verbal assault. I've come to regard it as Luca's defence when he is cornered. His blatant lies are less easy to condone. Unfortunately for him, we now have a new security system and his actions, if not witnessed at the time, are recorded for posterity.

He has another foible in that he considers himself something of a horticultural expert. He took it upon himself to prune a small tree, one of two that was potted and growing either side of our front entrance. I don't know what came over him, but when the concierge had gone home one evening he came downstairs and clipped the tree to within an inch of its life. The second tree, on the other side of the main door, remained untouched. The evening porter was on duty at the time but being small in stature and much shorter than Luca, was afraid to confront him. Next morning the concierge returned and, rightly furious, reprimanded both of them. With Luca, there was a shouting match, Luca venting and cussing ad-lib. Perhaps, by pruning the tree, he thought he had been helping. Definitely he didn't take kindly to being admonished. The decimated tree, not surprisingly, had to be replaced.

More recently, Luca's *odeur corporelle* left much to be desired. I thought he was ill. There was talk he was incontinent, a distasteful subject but, when you live in a block of flats, it is something that has to be addressed when it affects other residents. Worse still, the carpet round the corner from his front door had to be replaced for reasons I don't need to tell. The concierge was duty bound to confront Luca when his personal hygiene fell below an acceptable level. He was banned from sitting on the newly upholstered lobby chairs and most residents gave him a wide berth. For his defence he sought help from the local council, but nevertheless received some sort of legal letter from an attorney acting on behalf of landlord and leaseholders. I was not party to the contents, but for a while it achieved the desired effect. Luca's apparel, no less bizarre, began to look cleaner. The sole beneficiary of this sorry episode was the local supermarket which enjoyed increased sales of air freshener, acquired as I later discovered both by staff *and* Luca.

When Luca, or more accurately we, first moved in to the building all those years ago, most of the flats were resident-owned. They've since changed hands and the majority are now held as private investments and rented out, often to young people, some from overseas. Now that I'm an older resident, I enjoy their coming and going, although it does mean that the annual Christmas party in the lobby is less well attended. Younger tenants rarely participate, no matter that invitations are pinned up on notice boards in both lifts. Luca also does not attend. He probably, and rightly, feels he would not be well received, although I have no doubt he would be afforded a more gracious degree of civility on account of the season. It is not, I am sure, that he lacks the nerve to attend. Nor is he averse to a glass of wine, because I once saw him sitting outside a nearby restaurant with a wine glass in front of him. Unfortunately, his poor personal hygiene at the time saw him ousted from the premises for fear he deterred other diners.

Luca's problems are ongoing. The other week the fire alarm sounded just after five in the morning. Some of us – and I can see there's a tragedy waiting to happen here – went downstairs and waited outside the front entrance as per general instructions. After a while it was apparent there was no fire. Somebody phoned the concierge at home and he gave instructions on how to turn off the alarm. The panel on the wall behind the front desk indicated the problem had emanated from the first floor and located the flat number. Without thinking who lived there, I went upstairs and knocked on the door. I knocked three times. Eventually the door opened a crack and there stood Luca. "Are you all right? I asked, concerned. "Yes, I'm fine," he said sweetly before pointing to the flat next door. "The problem's in there," he said, jabbing a finger in the direction of another flat. I didn't quibble and he quickly closed the door. I had been too focussed on his nails which were ingrained with dirt that I failed to see beyond him to any possible signs of hoarding.

A much younger Asian resident who was renting opposite Luca had followed me up the stairs and stood behind me. When Luca closed his door, she told me quietly that nobody was living in the flat he had indicated. "Not for several months," she assured me. Later I learnt from the concierge that Luca sometimes sprayed the corridor with air-freshener, probably to mask any odour seeping out from his flat. It seems the spray had set off the alarm. When I questioned if this was feasible, I was assured it was, particularly if the aerosol spray was directed towards the alarm. "I did notice a sweet smell outside his door," I agreed. "But why would he spray outside and at such an hour?" The concierge shrugged. "I'll be having a word with him," he said ominously. And I didn't blame him. Living off premises, he had had to jump in his car and come straight over. Not only had other residents been raised from their beds, one had called the local fire department, which brought out a vehicle in a hail of sirens. Their time was also wasted.

Close surveillance of the CCTV camera erected near Luca's door (an action determined by the concierge, such is Luca's infamy) later revealed that Luca had indeed taken *two* cans of aerosol and pitched them in the direction of the alarm. He may have been trying to preserve his dignity, or hide an offensive odour, but he caused a chain of events that should never have occurred. He also flagrantly lied to me.

And that, unfortunately, is not all. Luca had, putting it politely, rigorously refused to leave a set of his keys in a locked cabinet with the concierge. The rest of us do on account of the fact it is easy to forget our personal keys and thereby lock ourselves out of our flats. On several occasions in the past Luca has done this to his cost, a locksmith having to come and assist him to gain entry again. You would think he would have learned from his mistake but no, he obstinately refused to hand over a spare set to the concierge for safekeeping.

Now, however, things have taken a slightly different course. Not long ago Luca disappeared for over a week. The staff assumed he had been admitted to hospital and grew concerned. Or could he, dread the thought, be in his flat unable to communicate or, worse still, have passed on? Local hospitals were called but, as we all know, gaining information when you are not a close relative is hard to achieve. Eventually the police came and they forced entry, whereupon the advanced state of hoarding was immediately confirmed. Indeed, they had difficulty locating the bathroom, let alone assuring themselves Luca was not present. Worse still, the flat was infested with bedbugs which set off a new train of action bringing in pest control, not only to Luca's flat but to those of his neighbours.

A new lock was installed, but this time it was of a certain type whereby it was known from the exterior whether or not anyone was within the flat at the time. Quite how it works is beyond me, but the police and the concierge, probably the landlord too, are in cahoots and it was deemed essential to protect all residents.

Luca had indeed been in hospital when all this occurred, but he returned seemingly improved and determined to continue his somewhat secretive life, apparently accepting that entry had been undertaken in his absence, and was content with the new lock that replaced the original. These days, he isn't seen very much. He is, as the concierge told me, keeping a low profile. Nobody knows where he goes. I returned from an evening soirée a few weeks ago just as he was going out, walking jauntily down the street wearing a strange ensemble highlighted by a gauze skirt to mid-calf and an outsized beige jacket.

So what will become of Luca? The Town Council and our landlord are, through their representatives, biding their time but as I'm reliably told *'carefully considering his case'*. As time goes by, will he become more morose or will he retreat into indifference and solitude? What if he was to write *his* memoir, how would it read? He most certainly must have had a life I know little about, cannot even guess at. Has he had lovers, male or female? I've only ever seen him once with one other person and that was at the time he was being refused permission to sit in the lobby. He was sitting outside a coffee shop having what looked like an urgent discussion with a lady whom I suspected might be a representative from the local council, perhaps a social worker.

Recently, and though still banned, he sat on one of our lobby chairs. When warned he was not permitted to do so, he moved to the porter's desk and pointedly announced he would be eighty-six in two weeks' time. Of course he could be lying (again) but this time I believe him because who among us claims an age higher than we look? Luca, despite his eccentric dress, doesn't look a day over eighty. Furthermore, he said he had had surgery to alleviate past problems pertaining to incontinence, thereby inferring that his right to sit on the chairs should be reinstated. For this to occur, and for him to be believed, he would undoubtedly have to produce a doctor's letter. It might also be pertinent for his flat to be checked to ensure the bathroom is fully functional and no longer overloaded with possessions.

To me, Luca has never been rude, quite the opposite. I leave it to you to determine if I should, and indeed could have done more as a longstanding neighbour. The world is full of eccentric characters and without them life would be boring. At times they cause havoc and upset, but beneath the subterfuge they are no less vulnerable than the rest of us. For now Luca continues going who-knows-where, catching buses, wearing his glitzy cap and mismatched socks, yet to me, when our paths cross, he remains unfailingly polite.

Palm Beach

Real estate – tunnels and hedges –
The Palm Beach Towers – Bernard

Much has been written about this small island enclave on the east coast of Florida. Three bridges join it to the mainland so it's a debatable point whether it can really be construed as an island. Nevertheless, the bridges are the link or the divider between two lifestyles. Those who live on the mainland tend to scoff, often disparagingly, at the fancy habits of Palm Beachers, while those who live on the island sigh gratefully at their enhanced security, met through local taxes.

Palm Beach contains some of the most expensive real estate in the United States. If it wasn't for the sprawling condominiums, this barrier island would almost certainly be the most expensive place to live, per square foot, in the country. I know because I was a resident living in a Palm Beach condominium for twenty-five years and I enjoyed the benefits paid for by owners of large homes, most of which fronted either the Atlantic Ocean or the Intracoastal Waterway separating Palm Beach from West Palm Beach. The island is only 18 miles (29 km) long and so narrow in places that it is possible to walk from the Ocean side to the Intracoastal, or vice versa, in about ten minutes.

Donald Trump, then a property developer/magnate, bought the estate known as Mar-a-Lago (meaning *sea to lake* in Spanish) towards the south end of the island, in 1985. It was originally owned and built (1924-7) by a cereal company heiress and socialite called Marjorie Merriweather Post. The entire estate extends over twenty acres and the main building covers more than 62,000sq feet. Trump elaborately refurbished and converted the property into a private club with high initiation fees and annual dues, and maintained one wing as his private residence.

While I lived in Palm Beach, I visited Mar-a-Lago many times. Two of these visits were to attend breakfast meetings of the local Chamber of Commerce and another occasion included an outdoor evening party celebrating the 100th anniversary of the town's incorporation on 17 April, 1911. It was during a further visit, when an indisposed resident gave me her ticket to a charity event, that I actually came face to face with The Donald, as he was then referred to, when he appeared halfway through the function to speak to some of the guests. He towered over a small throng who were asking questions while I stood back, hesitant to get involved. When he had had enough and was preparing to leave, he extended his hand through those he had been speaking to, and shook mine. "I'm Donald J. Trump, welcome to Mar-a-Lago, have a great evening," he boomed. A moment later, he turned about and left the room, bodyguards in hot pursuit. My surprise was not so much that he had determined to shake *my* hand but that he had chosen to shake any hand at all. Until then I had always thought he was a germaphobe with an aversion to unnecessarily touching others.

I went to Mar-a-Lago twice more to interview members of staff for articles I was writing for a local magazine. On one occasion I had to root out the history of the island's underground tunnels, one of which had been built by Mrs. Post and later renovated by Trump.

Private tunnels beneath many of the larger homes on the ocean side of the island were said to have been built so that local residents could reach the beach without crossing the street running beside the ocean. Nobody knew how many tunnels existed along this exalted stretch of real estate; the Town Building Department claimed there were fifteen but one knowledgeable local historian alleged there were twenty-four. How and why they came to be built was also open to conjecture. As I walked through some of these eerie looking passageways, tales of past intrigue regularly surfaced, not least from the staff at Mar-a-Lago. There it was suggested that perhaps they were used to transport forbidden booty to local homes during the time of Prohibition (1920-1933). Other residents spurned such an idea and feigned never to have heard it. Adding to the mystique and energising the rumour was the fact that some home-owners guarded their tunnels protectively and were reluctant to allow strangers in to see them. Among those I was allowed to view, some had fallen into disrepair. Although pumps had been used to clear seawater when it flooded in, there were unsightly damp brown patches covering the walls, and the entrances were sometimes clogged with sand.

Despite occasional flooding, the refurbished tunnel at Mar-a-Lago was immaculately maintained. The well-lit passage, built by Marjorie Post in the '20s and painted cream, had a serviceable but well trodden grey-blue flooring. I was assured its sole use now was so members of the club could reach the private beach and not have to cross the street. One member of staff, however, insisted on throwing a little pepper on the past. Although Mrs. Post was teetotal, she had been Queen of Palm Beach, throwing wild parties and masquerade balls. How, I was asked, could she have been elevated to the epitome of social thrones *without* offering her guests aperitifs and a glass or two of champagne? Impishly, this employee offered another dash of spice. "She also had a room in the basement with a false wall. You go through a narrow passage to reach it. It has no windows and would be a perfect place to store...."

The truth may never be known. Whether the tunnel was first and only used by bathers, or whether long ago it did double duty with furtive deliveries after dusk, remains uncertain. Certainly, if one takes a closer look at the period, then the rumours could be more than mere speculation and have substance. Remember the roaring Twenties, that profligate era of the 'rumble seat,' F. Scott Fitzgerald's *Jazz Age*, and the 'new woman' with her bobbed hair, short dresses and exotic dances? It was an exuberant era in the United States when freewheeling spirit led to wild new dances like the Charleston, and women shed their long Victorian underwear and first donned shorter skirts. The only cloud on this bawdy horizon was a national ban on the sale and manufacture of 'intoxicating liquor'. With overall prosperity, boosted by a roaring economy and a booming stock market, only the most virtuous citizens resolved to shun the demon drink, while numerous others found devious ways to outwit the law.

For Palm Beachers, the thought of sipping chaste beverages such as iced tea or coconut milk could well have presented a dilemma of nightmarish proportions. The thought of birthday celebrations without a toast or New Year's revelry without champagne was bad enough, but what about tender dinner dates with no Bordeaux or Chardonnay? Prohibition, inspired by temperance gangs, stirred high ideals but also roused flagrant disobedience. For the rich there were 'speakeasies', those select private clubs requiring a code-word entry and a vow of silence within. The risk of being discovered tainted the thrill for all but the most hardened patrons, so how much more discreet it would have been to have illicit plunder delivered home under cover of darkness and via a secret entrance.

Palm Beach has tales galore and more are sure to follow. Donald Trump will add to them, although they are unlikely to be linked to alcohol as he claims never to imbibe. During his presidency, neighbours were sorely tested with his regular visits to the island to play golf, fundraise or entertain other Republican politicians. The closing of roads when his entourage passed to and fro caused lengthy disruption and dismay, exacerbated by the sound of planes as air traffic passed overhead from Palm Beach International Airport. In the past, Trump had tried but failed to have the flight path changed and today, no longer president, he suffers the further indignity of his plane being forced to wait in line on any local runway.

Rumour, parties and presidents apart, what is never in dispute is the beauty of Palm Beach. Carefully manicured lawns and hedges, along with numerous types of palm trees, give the town a majestic look and have made it a much sought after hotspot for wealthy winter 'snowbirds' who come south before Christmas and fly back to their northern homes around Easter. The larger mansions, owned by entrepreneurs, artists and musicians, technology whizz-kids, writers and fashion designers, are discreetly shielded by high hedges, some of which have grown to Amazonian proportions. Every year town authorities send out inspectors who order reticent owners to cut these surrounds if they restrict the view of passing motorists.

The extent to which some residents go to enclose their homes and gardens knows no bounds. Some hedges are clearly more resplendent than others, hinting of oneupmanship but certainly adding to the town's overall charm and eccentricity. Two-tier hedges, with high ficus trees at the rear and smaller plants in front, is one impressive variation. A split-level hedge, separated by a low white fence or wall, is another. Other homeowners, determined not to be outdone, paint their window shutters the same shade of pinkish red as the flowers that bloom in their hedge. While an artistically clipped hedge with mushroom caps or balls ingeniously cut out on top, could earn an owner points for creative endeavour, too much eye-catching appeal is unacceptable. As one local landscape architect of animal and bird-shaped bushes once told me: "Best leave those for Disney World."

Given Florida's climate and rainfall, hedges of any type or height are neither cheap to plant nor to maintain. We're talking big bucks. For some local residents, however, the cost of growing and maintaining a hedge is superfluous. They will shell out at least two hundred thousand dollars (£150,000) a year on maintenance and upkeep of their gardens. Given this type of outlay, a few thousand on a hedge is neither here nor there. And as for the many visitors who yearn to peer in, they should dream to be birds. I've long thought there could be no better place to nest than in the elevated green surrounds of a secluded Palm Beach hedge with an unparalleled view of both sides.

Despite the winter season of charity balls and private parties, many residents live quietly in Palm Beach and rarely if ever participate in the social whirl. They endeavour not to be photographed or mentioned in *The Palm Beach Daily News* and take pleasure in tending their gardens themselves. They may or may not join one of several clubs on the island but they generally keep a low-key almost reclusive lifestyle from December through March. Nevertheless, in the many years I lived on the island, some sort of scandal broke almost every year; it could involve any resident be they young or old, rich or not so rich, eccentric or reclusive. Sometimes word escaped involving a licentious affair between socialites who took winter partying beyond the pale; or there was a jewellery heist; or a well-heeled resident was arrested for a misdemeanour or something more serious. The high heat and humidity seemed to inspire scandal, much of it untrue, but ever more colourful and occasionally involving sexual deviancy. One summer there was also a disturbing murder, which had the most sedate residents walking or cycling the trail around the island in a state of shock and speculation. When the culprit, not an islander, was eventually apprehended and put away, there was a collective sigh of relief.

One of the worst scandals would undoubtedly have to be the manner in which Jeffrey Epstein, billionaire financier and convicted sex offender, used his Palm Beach home for sex trafficking of minors, many of whom were molested or raped. At least two local police officers endeavoured, at personal risk to themselves and their careers, to have him convicted of serious charges, but money spoke louder than words and it was some years later before he was finally arrested for sex trafficking and died in prison awaiting trial.

Another resident with a Palm Beach bolt hole was Bernie Madoff, who ran the biggest Ponzi scheme in US history. He came to Palm Beach and conned many residents out of significant funds, causing heartache, tears, and wrenching of hands. He too ended life in prison.

The one-bedroom apartment where I lived was within a sprawling mid-town condominium on the Intracoastal side of Palm Beach. The building included a large heated outdoor pool surrounded by cabanas, which were owned and used by individual residents for card parties or backgammon, or simply to provide a vantage point from which to watch the antics in the pool. Each owner was responsible for the decor of their cabana, and these ranged from flat strewn red-striped Americana to more sedate sea blue tones with shell-encrusted draperies and framed prints of Florida. Every cabana owner I knew was passionate about their little retreat and not even the perennial problem of insects and legless reptiles deterred them.

The *Palm Beach Towers* had six floors, divided into two parts connected with through corridors on the mezzanine, ground and lower-ground floors. There was a large undercover entrance with valet parking and 24 hour reception. The mezzanine floor included a variety of offices and a dental surgery. On the two lowest floors there were more offices including a boutique bank, hairdressing salon, a tailor, a shop for basic groceries and a public restaurant. For residents' use only, there was a meeting room on the lower floor which doubled as a cinema, a library, and a fitness centre alongside changing rooms for the pool.

Whenever a new enterprise opened an office in the building, the venture would host some sort of event by which they introduced themselves to residents. I remember a local bank opening a small boutique branch on the ground floor and holding a lavish breakfast in the lobby. At the time I wondered how many more banks were needed before Palm Beach was officially declared to have more banks per head of population than elsewhere in the United States. Also, drawn by local wealth, competition was becoming increasingly fierce.

The week before I received an invitation to this particular breakfast, I received another from my own bank, which had a branch along the road from the condominium. With two invites in hand, I knew there was more to each occasion than welcoming me in for a friendly chat, but undeterred I accepted both. As a client, I first walked along the road to attend my bank's comparatively modest help-yourself occasion, and tucked into croissants and coffee, pastries and a few spaced-out strawberries. The branch manager came round and introduced herself, but for the most part I was left to nibble or eat for the day. Of those attending, most were already customers, many from my building, so there was no need for sales spiel. Furthermore, between neighbours there were plenty of asides from those who knew what was afoot and guessed we were being soft-soaped on account of approaching competition. When someone boldly asked if I would switch banks, I swore I would stay loyal unless confronted with ethical wrongdoing or gross mismanagement.

Unfortunately, ideals of a high order are easily expressed, but applying them is another matter. Nevertheless, it seemed socially legitimate to attend the second breakfast without incurring a conflict of ethics. Besides, this one had come from the president/CEO and the board of directors, inviting me personally to join them for the occasion. I will admit that while breakfast invitations were never my raison d'être, habits are quickly formed. I'm also an early riser and there was no distance to go.

By choosing to hold a party, complete with manifesto of services, in a spacious lobby a few strides from its new office, there was space as well as appeal. And the lobby being only a few strides from the new office was, to say the least, a shrewd move. Even more importantly, this breakfast was an upmarket feast; hot quiche, bread rolls and pastries, oodles of fresh fruit salad, cheese and spreads, and lots more. There was an excellent turn-out and the dive for the buffet was unrestrained. It was later rumoured that a few gluttonous residents had had the gall to arrive early for the pick of the table.

There were ladies to serve and clear, and smiling bank officials greeting you in a wondrous spirit of bonhomie that made one burn, temporarily anyway, with chivalrous intent to reciprocate. By the time the bank president spoke, we were putty in his hands. Did he take advantage? Well, not at first. Naturally, he was excited about the new enterprise and hoped we'd take a minute or two to survey the services offered. He warmed the cockles of our hearts by promising faithfully to be a good neighbour. He spoke for four minutes, just long enough for us to take a break before eating more.

The moment he finished, one resident assailed him in a frenzy that left boldness behind. She really thought, and suggested quite bluntly, that he should do the breakfast over again on a more regular basis. Those of us more modestly inclined looked askance, although we privately acknowledged her need. The dear lady had just undergone more than one bout of major surgery, and it was gratifying to see her appetite was back with a vengeance.

How one deals with such a question inevitably distinguishes a President from a president. Did our new neighbour laugh sickly and utter a faltering "Maybe"? Did he throw up his hands good-humouredly and appeal to the rest of us with a look that begged sympathy. Definitely not. With admirable panache and the speed of a born entrepreneur, he responded with a riposte that made the Play of the Day. Beaming broadly, he not only assured her he would do it again but next time we'd all have champagne! There was a yelp of appreciation and a round of applause. And, yes, just possibly a few million or more in business.

By the time I left, customers were lined up outside the new office. I tried telling myself I could salve my conscience by keeping an account with both banks, but deep down there was more to it than that. The ugly truth became apparent that the higher I strive to be principled, the more undignified my descent when I fail. In this case, there was the disquieting knowledge that I might be bought with a slice of quiche and the promise of champagne.

The condominium had other advantages. Not only was it a full-service building but the position, mid-island, made it much envied and sought after. Also, about fifteen minutes' walk south down the bicycle trail lay a wonderful complex known as The Society of the Four Arts. I was never a member (there was a waiting list of years) but each winter I attended films and direct opera telecasts from the Metropolitan Opera in New York. Occasionally I was also invited as a guest to hear illustrious speakers from all over the US.

It was close to this complex one Saturday morning when I first encountered another resident from my condominium, an older gentleman who had a special interest in interiors and culture. At the time we were participating in an event arranged by The Four Arts, whereby several nearby homes opened their doors to benefit a children's charity. Our tickets enabled us to enter each home and admire the contents as well as the gardens.

His name was Bernard. He was slim, immaculately dressed, and very particular. "Julia, it is not Bernard," he soon corrected me. "My name is pronounced Ber-NARD."

A few days later he invited me to his annual Christmas Eve party. He called me on the In-House phone and explained that every year he invited guests to a dinner in his apartment and would be pleased if I would attend. No sooner did I accept than he asked me what I would wear. "What would you like me to wear?" I countered, taken aback. I had realised by then that he was a man of fastidious taste and I was already concerned that I might not rise to his expectation.

"Something festive," he announced. "Not black. And don't be late."

Fortunately I owned a red cocktail dress with frills at the hem. I thought it would be appropriate.

The evening came and I knocked on his door at two minutes past seven, the anointed hour. Not surprisingly, I was the first to arrive. Bernard opened the door, surveyed me from top to toe and smiled benignly. I took this to mean I had passed the test of appearance, and followed him through the vestibule into the living room. Jack, his partner, was working in the kitchen assisted by two ladies dressed to serve and clear. Three or four card tables were set against a wall, all closed but draped with folded tablecloths, ready for dinner.

I placed my handbag on an unencumbered chair and studied a cabinet full of precious cut glass bowls and antique napkin rings. Moments later I looked at the chair and saw my bag was gone. Handbags, I soon realised were not permitted on chairs within the living room. That evening, as other guests began arriving and Bernard went to greet them, I saw they laid their bags beside mine which then rested on a banquet table the other side of the entrance. From that evening on, I knew always to place my handbag there.

When a home is *very* full of artefacts, whether they cover walls, are displayed in cabinets or arranged on top of a black Bosendorfer baby grand, it is difficult to know where to look first and harder still to know what to say. On my first visit to Jack and Bernard's apartment, there was also an overloaded Christmas tree in one corner, with all manner of ornaments and beautifully wrapped gifts beneath. I soon discerned that Bernard was the collector while Jack shouldered the homely virtues and was, for the most part, the quieter of the two. Years later it was Jack who confided to me that he considered Bernard's prolific 'collecting' an illness. I don't know that I would have gone that far but certainly amassing so many objects, be they antique or not, was Bernard's passion and he neither could nor would relinquish it.

His eclectic taste stretched from antique opaline eggs and vases in various colours to articulated silver fish and crystal theatrical tiaras believed to have been worn by opera divas at La Scala. There was German gold-decorated porcelain, Waterford crystal pitchers from Ireland, and an Italian chandelier. Beside a red lacquer screen from India stood camel side tables made out of teak and lacquered white, and an entire cabinet housing a collection of silver-capped French perfume bottles. For this evening only, the piano lid was raised and the top unencumbered; usually a collection of small sphinxes in basalt, bronze and Baccarat crystal were precisely positioned on top.

Bernard was unabashed about how his passion began. Once a fashion coordinator and window dresser for a major New York store, he toured Europe in his spare time, scouting out useful items in flea markets and antique stores. When I met him he was already eighty, and the ability to travel and acquire pieces was restricted by mobility problems, but he was still driven.

Jack, while not complicit in the collecting had, possibly unwittingly, contributed to the mind-blowing array of items displayed. He enjoyed needlepoint and was responsible for an embroidered pillow of a whippet on a damask striped sofa beneath two painted canvas panels surrounded in malachite. A framed needlepoint of a bowl of flowers, also by Jack, hung on a far wall above two of the unique camel side tables which stood beside a pair of richly upholstered Venetian chairs.

The living room of this two-bedroom apartment resembled a museum. If somewhat daunting at first view, the vibrant colours and meticulous placing of pieces always made visiting an experience, particularly as Bernard was happy to talk about his treasures, their history, and how and where he came to acquire them. When he first saw my home, I think he was a little disappointed that I had a preference for modern furnishings and he took it upon himself to educate me about antiques.

Every year Bernard invited me to accompany him to one or more of the annual antique and jewellery shows in West Palm Beach. These were usually held in large marquees during January or February, and he invariably received invitations to attend. Jack sometimes accompanied us, but he was equally content to stay at home and let Bernard escort me. I knew to dress elegantly for these occasions and often felt that Bernard secretly hoped it gave rise to the misconception that we were a couple and that he was with a considerably younger lady. He exuded an air of authority and knowledge, expecting dealers to dance attendance and consider him a potential buyer, when in fact he had no intention of paying the inordinate sums required for many of the items. He would quietly yet audibly murmur to me about such-and-such a piece and how it might look in such-and-such a position, inferring to onlookers that we not only shared a home but had space, and were indeed looking for, a certain piece to fill it. Sometimes he told me to enter individual stands, either to ask a question or to discreetly turn a small label and ascertain price. At all times he maintained an air of superiority, speaking earnestly yet in muted tones as he surveyed exhibits with an expert eye, carefully discerning desirable items from those unworthy of his attention.

With shows including fine jewellery, Bernard was not averse to playing a little joke, and one particular afternoon he excelled himself. He told me to take his arm shortly before entering the curtained stand of one of the world's most esteemed gem dealers. I guessed something was afoot but we were already being welcomed within so it was too late to refuse. After shaking hands with the manager, Bernard asked to see a whopping green diamond ring which had been rivetingly displayed in the firm's recent advertising. Not willing to miss a potential buyer, and few people had the gall to enter the inner sanctum without serious interest, we were requested to sit on two plush red chairs in front of a low counter while the assistants bustled about, slightly agitated but clearly eager. Soon enough the diamond ring appeared on a velvet-covered tray with at least two suited gentlemen, presumably security, taking up positions by the curtained entry. By now my heart and brain were reacting with a sense of foreboding and stress. Not only did I know that Bernard had no intention whatsoever of buying the bauble, either for me or as the pièce-de-résistance in his collection, I knew I was about to be embarrassed by a further factor; I had omitted to have a manicure.

"Try it on!" came the united appeal of the assistants. Bernard studied the ring and indicated his approval with a short nod.

I took the exquisite ring, placed it quickly on the ring finger of my right hand, scrunched up my fingers so that my nails were obscured, and extended my hand towards Bernard and those who were watching. Of course there were admiring gasps from the ladies while the salesmen beamed. I smiled modestly, muttered something about the beauty of the diamond and its setting, and waited for Bernard's next move.

"No," he said sighing a little. "It's the wrong colour. Yellow would be better. Do you have a yellow diamond, the same size or larger?"

The staff looked crestfallen. The man in charge was not done. "We do indeed have a yellow diamond, Sir, in New York. We could have it here in 48 hours or perhaps less, if you would be interested?"

By this time, Bernard was rising from his chair. There was a short discussion on the weight, the carats and the value of the yellow diamond. "Let me think about it," was Bernard's final remark. "I could be interested. May I have your card?"

Twenty seconds later we were through the curtains and back on the carpeted corridor that extended the length of the marquee between the stands. As we walked on towards the next section, my heart rate began to fall.

"How could you?" I said at length, smiling nervously, suppressing a laugh.

Bernard smiled smugly and stared straight ahead. "I want to look at some vintage French sconces," he said earnestly, refusing to be drawn on the matter.

Men

The infamous one – mistaken identity – the greatest compliment – the measure of a man

In Palm Beach I once had an older admirer called Lawrence. Our platonic friendship extended over some years until he reluctantly accepted that I was not interested in moving to the next level, and he married a wealthy lady nearer his own age who better appreciated his whacky charm. The truth was that Lawrence came to the island specifically to find a rich wife and eventually succeeded. At first he entertained hopes of courting me (he liked the idea of my having a pied-à-terre in London), but I gently dissuaded him (I wasn't rich enough) and we struck up a mutually advantageous friendship.

When we first met he was busy attending the social whirl of parties prevalent in the town during the winter. His diary of engagements was heavily booked because there was a shortage of single men who knew how to treat a lady and he was a reliable escort not deeply attached to any one in particular. He escorted a range of older women who were either divorced or widowed and who needed a partner (known locally as a 'walker') to attend charity balls. They bought the tickets while Lawrence, having leased a good car and knowing how to dress, was happy to accompany them. The ladies were content because he drank very little and was thereby unlikely to embarrass them, and could drive them home at the end of the evening. Furthermore, he dressed and behaved appropriately, was reliably punctual and made amusing small talk. He was also tall, looked younger than his years and knew how to dance without treading on toes. He once admitted to me that he had been on a number of cruises, earning a reduced ticket as a dancing partner for single ladies.

Lawrence referred to his social commitments as 'formals' and told me he had three tuxedos (dinner jackets) and they were rotated in turn, with two in action and one at the dry cleaners. Every now and again, however, he needed a break from the hectic social round and would call me to say how much he would appreciate a home-cooked dinner, for which he would bring wine and after which he would happily take me to a movie. Very often he let me choose the film, presumably because he had not had time to see what was showing locally. Sometimes I chose movies that did not interest him, or after so many late nights he was too exhausted to enjoy, and he nodded off during the performance.

One evening I suggested a movie and forewarned him that it was a foreign film with subtitles. Just so he knew, I added in passing that the review said the movie contained some nudity. Far from being deterred, Lawrence was all for going to the earliest performance and I found myself preparing dinner halfway through the afternoon. We still managed to cut it fine and arrived with little time to spare. Lawrence showed less concern than usual parking his car and, despite a pulled hamstring, had the tickets in two minutes flat.

We sat down a little breathless just as the movie began. Throughout the film, my friend sat bolt upright and never once looked likely to doze. At the end I couldn't help but be pleased. "You know," I told him. "I think that's the first film I've seen where the only bit of nudity involved a man."

Lawrence, who seemed altogether disappointed with the show, looked incredulous. "You know I didn't notice any nudity – was there some?"

"At the beginning," I told him laughing. "Surely you remember?"

He did not. "You know what your trouble is," I said. "You can't bear to think that the only nudity was related to a man, so you've blocked it out of your mind!" Though crestfallen, he was honest enough to admit that could be so.

Next morning he called me and it seemed his memory had returned. Overall, he thought the movie contained little of substance and while he did now remember that particular scene, he failed to see the significance of it in the story. I agreed. "Frankly," I told him, "I thought it was not only irrelevant but in poor taste. Anyway, I don't know why the director bothered because there was nothing special about it. You're all made alike." When he started to pick up on that last remark, I hastily changed the subject.

If nothing else, Lawrence wouldn't give up. Soon afterwards he determined on a more irreverent plan to gain my affection. Some would describe it as shocking but I've learned, whenever possible, to handle the outrageous by dismissing it as of no importance or laughing it off as absurd.

While Lawrence knew better than to push his luck, one evening he sank to a new low. My birthday was approaching and he told me he wanted to bring me a gift. As a token of thanks, I invited him once more to dinner.

While I was in the kitchen, he went to use the bathroom. A couple of minutes later he emerged, calling out in excitement that I should come and claim my gift. When I entered the lounge, he advanced towards me stark naked with a tennis bracelet hanging from you-know-where...

I've always believed that in extreme moments like this it is incumbent upon a lady to stay calm and inhale deeply while maintaining a (mostly) straight face. I approached him, whipped off the bracelet, thanked him kindly and then told him to put his clothes back on before I served dinner. The meal continued and, yes, we remained friends. Sometime later I donated the bracelet to a charity shop.

* * *

Let's face it, some men are incorrigible. They want what they want and are prepared to pay for it. And in their eagerness, they sometimes err and retreat red-faced. Years ago it happened twice. Fortunately I came to no harm and in the second instance even felt some compassion for circumstances surrounding their approach.

In London, around 1980 or shortly thereafter, when I had bought and moved into my little flat, I began to have unexpected male visitors pressing my doorbell at odd times of the day and evening. Security and the means to enter the building were less strict than today; staff came and went, the front entrance door was sometimes left open, tradesmen did not sign in and it was many years before CCTV was invented, let alone installed. Whenever a visitor arrived, they were supposed to press the exterior bell to announce they were there and then wait to be admitted. Unfortunately there were occasions when they walked straight in without permission and this regrettably led to at least one serious assault on an elderly resident.

The chance callers who pressed my button all asked for the same lady they thought lived in my flat. When I told them they must have the wrong number, they usually disappeared. On one occasion a man made it to my door and I foolishly opened it. He took one look at me, realised his mistake, and scurried back to the lift with a mumbled apology in his wake. Before long, the penny dropped as to what these erstwhile visitors were after. I went down to the lobby one afternoon and met the resident porter who was in the throws of entertaining two uniformed police officers over a cup of tea. I explained the situation and floated the possibility there was a local call-girl in a nearby building, with the same flat number as mine. "Say no more, Ma'am," one officer replied. "We'll take care of it." And take care of it he did. The incidental visits ceased and my doorbell no longer rang at inopportune moments.

This was the first of two occasions when I was mistaken for a hooker. On neither occasion was it related to how I dressed or behaved, although in the second instance my hair colour played a significant role. I was modestly attired and used no tactic that could have have been construed as enticing.

The second time I was the direct recipient of unwanted advances. It happened some years later when I was living in a poor country badly stricken by poverty and disaster. My fair hair and complexion vaguely likened me to prostitutes who came south, crossing the border from alien parts, particularly at weekends. Together we were easily distinguishable from the local population who to a person were olive-skinned and dark haired. This time the errors usually occurred on Saturday afternoons when, weather permitting, it seemed like every man in the country went walking or driving. While I dressed carefully, and in a manner which by British standards could be considered conservative, this was not sufficient to prevent my being singled out and approached.

The preamble to each proposition was much the same. A young man would appear beside me and politely engage me in conversation. I knew enough of the local language to converse on a superficial level and answered questions when asked how long I had been in the country, did I like it and where I came from. After a minute or two, the realisation dawned on my interrogator that he might – no probably had – made a gaffe of monstrous proportion. My nationality was not what he had anticipated and I was not steering the conversation towards financial remuneration for services to be rendered. When I told him the nature of my business and that I was simply out for a walk, I threw the ball in his court.

At this point the would-be clients reacted differently. Some promptly took off, disappearing shamefaced down the nearest side street never to be seen again. Others, more audacious, determined to brazen it out. One young man, when he realised his mistake, bowed low, seized my hand and kissed it respectfully. It was, he assured me, a pleasure to know me and if at any time he could be of service, it would be his highest wish....*Quite!* I thanked him politely and accepted the card he offered. We parted all smiles and that was the last I saw of him.

The medal for Most Shameless Conduct went to another. This time, once the man acknowledged his error, he announced that his mother was an excellent cook and asked if I would do him the honour of having dinner one night at his parents' home. Frankly, I doubt I could have looked his mother in the eye. There was also the unsettling thought that, while he did not know it, I was possibly old enough to *be* his mother! In this country women had a hard life; the standard of living was low, their homes were frequently without water and electricity, and city air was badly polluted. They had no access to quality cosmetics or knowledge of a healthy diet. Added together, these factors contributed to early ageing.

I'm sure this young man would have taken me to his parents' home because local custom required that visitors be greeted, welcomed and entertained. Also, he almost certainly lived with his parents because in the capital where I lived, housing was limited and nearly all young people stayed with their parents until, and often long after, they married. There was a long waiting list for housing of any kind.

As with the rest, I never saw the man again, nor did I meet his parents. His impudent conduct told me he would go far; my only concern was in which direction.

* * *

To several men I attribute a great deal of happiness. They have lifted me up, made me laugh and astonished me. There have been times when one or two have made me furious or weep with frustration and loss but, taken as a whole, they have added colour and fun and ecstasy to my life. Some have left an indelible impression and the nefarious deeds of a few have been offset by the kindness and wicked good humour of others. They have shown me places I otherwise would never have seen, introduced me to sports I knew little about, and made comments I've carried with me and treasured long afterwards. I may have known them for years or met them fleetingly, but they left a lasting impression.

One man, who paid me a memorable compliment, I never really knew. I was in my early thirties and had just resettled in London after some years in Australia. I had taken part-time work pulling beers in a local pub and would rise early, write for a few hours, then head off to oversee the lunchtime shift at the pub, Monday through Friday. I thought working in such an environment would provide grist for the mill and be entertaining; I was not disappointed.

The pub was close to a school and a police station, and several times a week the headmaster of the school came in for a half pint, sometimes accompanied by the school janitor. Police officers also frequented the place but mostly in the evenings. One might have expected their presence, even off duty, to instil a sense of decorum, but this was not always the case. While lunchtimes usually saw better behaviour, evenings sometimes brought trouble. I once arrived shortly before noon to find the manager sporting a nose the size and colour of an aubergine. During some sort of contretemps the previous evening, he had misjudged the distance between himself and a belligerent patron, and received a direct hit to the face and with it a broken nose.

The school janitor was one of several Irishmen who regularly sat at the bar. His brother, a mysterious character straight out of D.H.Lawrence, would occasionally join him before disappearing as mysteriously as he arrived. Nobody knew what the janitor's brother did or where he came from, and the janitor never let on. There were rumours, possibly hearsay, that his brother made routine visits to the Emerald Isle and was involved in questionable deals. Occasionally the brothers sat side by side at the bar but more often than not the janitor's brother stayed alone at a table towards the rear of the saloon and observed the room in private. He was a man of few words and with his thick black beard was slightly intimidating. Even so, he was always polite to me and sometimes revealed a mischievous sense of humour. For most of the time, however, he sat with a pint of beer, saying little, merely indicating with a nod of his head when he wanted another.

One Friday, towards the end of my shift and not long before I gave up the job, some of the patrons clubbed together and presented me with a coupon to help towards an air ticket for my next trip. The janitor's brother was there and instead of sitting at the back of the room, he took a seat at the bar. When the bell for last orders sounded, he nodded towards his glass and I moved to draw him another. With perfect timing, he leant towards me and in his glorious Irish brogue, whispered unexpectedly and to lasting effect. "You know," he said quietly, "that I'd mortgage my soul to spend the weekend with you." Forty years have passed but the thought has not lost its lustre. That he never did is immaterial.

* * *

Finally, let's talk the measure of a man whose thanksgiving service I recently attended at The Guards' Chapel in London's Wellington Barracks. Garry was a neighbour of mine and we first met in 2015 when I was in the throws of moving back to London from the United States. He was then living in a ground floor bedsit flat and his exuberance to meet me was tinged with mischief. He presumably recognised a fellow traveller, better still a female, coming home to roost and wanted to introduce himself. We soon came to an arrangement whereby we met regularly every few weeks, his place or mine, meeting early evening to split a bottle of red and discuss the perils of the day. At first he took the stairs from his flat on the ground floor to mine on the fourth, arriving slightly out of breath. "Missing part of a lung," he panted. "But I need the exercise." In fact, he was not only missing part of a lung but as a result of a first stroke had lost his sight to the point he was legally blind. Outdoors he used a white cane but never let it deter him. He sometimes rode a scooter in the park and worked out on an exercise machine squeezed into his small flat. From old photos, I could see he remained lean and trim his entire life.

At the time Garry was still travelling and took off twice a year to stay with friends in the south of France or Thailand. One evening he told me that he would like to have a budgerigar and he was hoping I might share responsibility and look after the bird when he was away. I reminded him that I was a traveller too and there could be a problem if our trips coincided, not to mention the fact that no pets of any type were permitted in the building. Undeterred, Garry presented me with a book on budgies and asked me to read it.

In fact I already knew quite a bit about the chatty little birds because my twin, Mary, had kept an aviary in a converted summerhouse in the garden of our childhood home. She began with one bird in a cage in our nursery and somehow gained another and the two begat many more. The room could no longer house them and they moved out into their own newly wired home beside the rockery garden. Golden pheasants arrived to share the ground terrain which extended outside over rocks and plants, leaving the budgies with the upper perches, always busy with an increasing number of breeding boxes.

I read the book and then told Garry that it could not be. I couldn't keep a budgie because they needed space to fly around and the advice was that any mirrors should be covered so that the bird could have daily exercise. I had floor to ceiling mirrors in two rooms, and others in the bathroom. Draping them would be impossible.

Garry took the news in his stride. He accepted too that his mobility was restricting his ability to travel and his trips became less frequent. Soon afterwards he suffered an incapacitating (second) stroke and spent a miserable year in and out of hospital followed by a further eighteen months in a nursing home. I thought of his passing as something of a relief. When a formerly very active man lies bedridden, unable to do anything for himself, there is a cruelty akin to a caged beast who cannot roam. Worse still, towards the end he grew a little muddled, although this might or might not have been due to the medication he was urged to take. Despite his confusion, whenever I went to see him he remained stoic and accepting, even making light of a dire situation. "You can come any time you want," he said once, a wry grin on his face. "I'm not going anywhere."

During his incarceration he never complained, never grew frustrated or angry. A superb athlete in his youth, he once qualified to train for the Olympics, competed in triathlons, and as a cyclist thought nothing of pedalling from London to France or Bangkok to Singapore. He had been an accomplished skier both on the slopes and barefoot over water. Last but not least, he had been an ardent tobogganist. Until the Thanksgiving Service, of all these physical pursuits, the only one he had ever told me about was how he had managed riders on the Cresta run, working for more than twenty years every winter at the St Moritz Tobogganing Club in Switzerland.

The staff in the hospital and the nursing home were astonished at the number of visitors he received. One afternoon when he was in hospital, he had so many people come to see him that I had to leave early. Not only was there a melee around his bed but another patient, presumably an inmate at a local penitentiary, had his own entourage of guards adding to the overcrowded ward. It was Piccadilly Circus at Christmas.

It wasn't until I listened to the eulogies that I had an inkling why Garry was so admired. The turn-out for the service hinted that this was no ordinary eighty-two year old man being politely remembered. Despite the pandemic, and it being a bleak mid-November day, at least two hundred showed up in the chapel.

As a young man Garry had been an officer in the Irish Guards before transferring to the Army Air Corps. This helped account for the chapel bristling with men, mostly older but including a few young Irish guardsmen in full dress uniform. The unit's mascot, an Irish wolfhound called Seamus, resplendent in a matching red jacket, stood by, suitably sombre under his burly handler's control.

According to the eulogist, Garry generated respect and affection from all ranks as a gifted pilot and instructor. "His bravery was legendary," we were told. "He went out on a prolific number or reconnaissance and rescue missions, fearless under enemy fire."

Very soon a picture emerged of a man who was not only talented and brave but had lived a peripatetic life, unable to stay too long in one place. Later he became a civilian rescue pilot in Hong Kong, the Middle East and over the North Sea. Ambition and wealth were never on his list of priorities and he was without ego.

Towards the end of the service the Last Post resounded down the aisle, the choir sang the Irish Blessing and Seamus filed out with his handler behind the senior chaplain. I imagined Garry smiling a little bemused at the crowd, and beaming merrily when he caught sight of two coaches waiting to take many of us to the wake at the Cavalry and Guards Club on Piccadilly. Garry loved a gathering and would have been delighted that his friends saw fit to meet up and celebrate his passing with a glass or two.

He was not a wealthy man, far from it; money would have hindered his free spirit and he never sought it other than to maintain his independence and to travel. At the service he was described as a nomad, seldom staying anywhere for more than three years. His only child, a daughter, described how, towards the end of his life when he was totally incapacitated, she had the chance to really get to know and love him. To her great credit she held no grudge for time lost, recalling only exciting times when as a teenager she rode pillion on his motorbike.

Garry was always upbeat, on the lookout for something to laugh about or a current event to discuss. Above all, he was generous to those he saw struggling or in dire straits through no fault of their own. When a young member of staff in our building fell seriously ill, it was Garry, although he could ill afford it, who promptly sent a gift in four figures.

The thanksgiving service not only celebrated his life, it honoured the measure of a man who valued loyalty and friendship over success; was gentle, spiritual and gallant. The sadness is that we don't always recognise, or not till it's too late, when we are in the company of someone who is heads above the crowd.

Life's a Production

On stage – words and worse – preparing to exit –
melodrama – starting over in London – another Act?

The first time I was asked to speak in public – and
for just two minutes – I panicked. The nearer the
time came to speak, the more concerned I became. Not
surprisingly, I sought advice. I was living in Florida and
on the day in question I took an early morning walk
before the sun grew hot and met a friend out doing the
same. In passing I told her I was nervous. "The trick is
not to look into the faces in front of you," was her advice.
"Look just over their heads."

This sounded like wise advice. The time came and with
a brief note in hand, I delivered my address. I thought it
went reasonably well but asked a member of the audience
for their honest opinion. "You were OK," came the
slightly perplexed reply. "But why were you staring at
the ceiling?"

With practice, I improved. My topic was usually
on being a global volunteer and how it came about,
beginning inevitably with life in Armenia. I will never be a
natural public speaker; I don't expect to have an audience
rolling in the aisles or sitting bolt upright, mesmerised
by my words. I did learn that preparation is key, along
with practising out loud, either alone or before a small
audience of friends.

I remember my first attempt but not much about the talks that followed. Americans have always seemed to me to have more confidence, something about their education encourages them to speak up, to have opinions and to be unafraid of voicing them. Some are openly eager to grab a microphone and start talking. We Brits, on the other hand, tend to employ wit and self-deprecation, and know the value of a well-timed pause for dramatic effect.

Public speaking wasn't the only hill I learnt to climb in the United States. Soon after I arrived and took residence there, I made several gaffes over words with different meanings. I messed up royally in Manhattan, where I first lived, committing a howler while assisting with the editing of one of my then-husband's compositions. Loris was and remains an eminent composer and conductor, criss-crossing the world for performances and the promotion of his work. On the afternoon in question, a young musician had come to our apartment to help with last minute changes to a new composition, and together the three of us sat around the dining-room table making alterations. In years to come computers would cut this tedious task, but at the time each member of the orchestra received a score laboriously copied by hand. Initial changes to players' parts were made in pencil and, after discussion, sometimes altered.

"Can I borrow your rubber?" I asked the young man assisting us. He paused, looked at me slowly and endeavoured not to smile. "You mean this?" he queried, holding up the article in question. "Here it is known as an eraser and you can *never* borrow a rubber!"

One prophylactic apart (although in American English the plural *rubbers* may refer to galoshes) other words caused less concern. To me certain American words seem to fit and sound better than their English counterparts, others less so. I have always preferred *cookies* to *biscuits; sweater* to *jumper* or *pullover; diaper* to *nappy; sidewalk* to *pavement;* and *poop* in place of *poo.* By comparison, I would opt for the British *zip* in place of *zipper; mean* over *stingy;* and *pub* over *bar.*

But events invariably overshadow words and, whether cruel or astonishing, some are impossible to forget. I was at boarding school in November, 1963 when the US President John F. Kennedy was assassinated, and I remember my headmistress walking sombrely down the aisle in the dining room where the whole school was sitting. A gong rang and silence descended as she stepped onto the platform beside the high table and picked up the microphone. Too young to fully comprehend the significance of the moment, her tone was sufficient to cast an indelible shadow and establish the memory.

An inspiring moment came when I worked for a family in the south of France and Neil Armstrong first walked on the moon. Watching the phenomenon unfurl on a specially rented television set in July, 1969, we all cheered, spellbound and excited. Years later and there followed another tragedy and an appalling attack. I had just finished entertaining in my Florida apartment when news came through that Princess Diana had been killed in a car crash in 1997. Finally, on 11 September, 2001, I was en route to the dentist when members of the Wahhabi terrorist group, better known as Al-Quaeda, attacked the United States. My appointment was delayed as I sat with my dentist in his office, watching the horror unfold.

Days of infamy come and go. Days of reflection leading to personal life-changing decisions are less easy to recall. There was no light-bulb moment when I determined that

I should return to live in Britain. The thought evolved slowly but irrepressibly, although in the beginning I never considered what would be involved or how long it would take.

I was in my mid-sixties when I floated the thought of leaving Florida, where I had been based for twenty years, and returning to London. My twin, Mary, had died of leukaemia a few years before, and perhaps her passing set off an alarm bell in my head that we are all mortal. We can tidy up loose ends or leave everything to chance and other people. I have known others say airily: "Who cares? I'll be gone. Not my concern." I have known men of my age who have sizeable assets in more than one country, who have not even made a will. I find their carelessness reprehensible, particularly if I know they have children who undoubtedly will be left to sort through the mess they leave behind. And by the time everything has been attended to over several years, and lawyers have unravelled and squabbled and charged exorbitant fees for handling the estate, not to mention governments claiming their cut, there might not be much left. How anyone who has worked hard for much of their life could readily shrug off the importance of putting their affairs in order, I have never understood.

When I first considered leaving the United States, I wondered if I was moving against the tide. The number of Brits returning to live in the United Kingdom fades into insignificance compared to the citizens who decamp and leave for sunnier climes, new jobs or to execute some nefarious escape. Friends on both sides of the Atlantic queried whether I could tolerate the climate in Britain after so long in Florida. I was sure, however, that easy access to a wealth of cultural events, as well as proximity to other parts of Europe, would offset climatic differences. More importantly, I have long felt that many people leave it too late before downsizing. They cling selfishly to the familiar and refuse to simplify their living arrangements and move closer to public transport, hospitals, shops and family. My family were all based in the UK and by moving I would have financial assets in one country.

I was fortunate to still own my tiny London flat. For years I had used it when returning to visit family, notably my mother. After she died, and as Florida became increasingly prone to hurricanes, I took to staying in it worry-free for a few weeks each year towards the end of summer. Now I saw it evolving once more, this time into my retirement home.

I shared my thoughts on returning permanently to London over a wine-filled lunch with my former British accountant. This set the cogs turning along with the realisation that moving back would not be as simple as I first thought. In fact there followed three years of sorting tax problems and paying sizeable fees to Uncle Sam (the US government took a cut on profits accrued over the years I was resident there).

Over the course of those next three years, I eliminated a huge amount of personal items (all those photographs!) and effects. Fortunately I'm no magpie, but nevertheless I had to ruthlessly discard reminders of the past. I sorted wardrobes and cabinets and threw out one or two bags every week with regimented determination. During each of my last few visits to London, I returned with a few sentimental knick-knacks and clothes, always mindful that my London flat was one-third the size of my home in Palm Beach.

Organising the clearing out of one home in one country and moving to another is not to be undertaken lightly or left too late. Early in the process, and as a preventative measure against stress, I paid for a shingles shot. I may never know if it was a wise investment, but I've known others in my family who have had the disease and suffered at length.

Now let's pause a moment to talk worry and stress. We all suffer from each at some point or other and moving home undoubtedly triggers one or both. In rational moments I make a careful distinction between the two. Unfortunately, when I worry, I either forget there is a difference or try to convince myself that I suffer from stress. 'Worry' is when my imagination latches onto concern and springs into overdrive, and 'stress' is when the problem is immediate, threatening and humourless. It is not that I ever have cause to worry, rather that it veers out of control or deviates from the focal point. Of the two, stress is by far the uglier. Stress is reality-based and causes sleepless nights. Endure it too long, and one or more parts of the body start to rebel. Unless you have ever suffered from real stress, you can have no idea which part of your system is going to revolt. If you want to discover the location of your Achilles heel, the best way I know is to have a serious cash-flow problem. Less money coming in than going out is guaranteed to upset a body's equilibrium. Because of stress, some people have ulcers; others fall prey to depression. In my case, my teeth start moving around in my mouth, my gums fester, and my periodontist starts sharpening his scalpel.

Worrying is altogether different. On the whole, I think women worry more than men – which might account for our having a greater reputation for talking about others and, just possibly, concerning ourselves with other people's affairs.

Worrying can also be motivated by selfishness and may career into melodrama. For example, I worry whenever I travel. Then my concern is, if I fail to come home, have I left anything embarrassing behind? Are there letters or diaries that reveal more of myself than I want others to discover? Dare I risk leaving them, or should I destroy them at three in the morning, a few hours before my departure?

I have a friend who told me she bothers about leaving certain items of clothing. She agonises over the thought that if she goes away and never returns, her friends will rummage through her drawers of intimate apparel and scoff as they work. I told her once that if she was so concerned, perhaps she should take an extra suitcase wherever she goes. That way, her lingerie stays or wastes with her!

We both know our worrying is largely overreaction, an innate tendency which we seem unable to control, to worry out of perspective. Moving, however, is undeniably stressful because it demands actions and attention to detail, along with the fear of making wrong decisions.

In my case I wanted a clean break, so I sold my Palm Beach apartment fully furnished, along with all intangible assets. I left some cash in a non-interest bearing account for any unforeseen costs and to have ready funds should I return to Florida to see friends. I had three paintings sent to London along with several bundles of US tax papers, the latter to be dutifully retained for seven years.

On the day I sold my American home, I moved into a local hotel overnight and invited friends in for a final drink in the lounge, close to the bar. At the end of the evening there were a few hugs and that was it. The following afternoon, with only hand luggage, I left the United States.

I flew from Miami on 30 June, 2015 and arrived next morning in London, a newly returned resident of Great Britain. A day or two later I returned my US Green Card (work permit) to the United States Embassy, together with a signed form of relinquishment.

You could say I was in something of a parlous state on arrival, but I caught my breath. At least I had a roof over my head. With so much to do, the priority was getting things in the right order and the first task was to obtain a recognised UK address. Until I had an official document from the local council with my name and residential address, I could not move on. While I had a flat to live in, and remained the registered owner, the local council retained my Florida address. The most urgent and compelling reason to have this changed was so that I could sign on to a medical practice. I waited impatiently for a fortnight, hoping nothing untoward would happen to me in the interim.

Another anxious wait ensued before the funds I transferred from America showed up here in my chosen account. It had taken some form filling (by me) to set the transfer in motion but needed only the press of a button (by the bank) to make the switch, yet amazingly it took the better part of a week before the funds appeared in my designated London account. I grudgingly accept that every enterprise is entitled to a little extra by way of interest on top of regular charges, but this added to my overall angst.

Once the local council confirmed my new residential address and the bank confirmed my nest egg had arrived,

I set out with renewed purpose. There followed a lot of walking between banks, doctors' surgeries, a new financial advisor, the library (for help in many matters) and more. Sometimes there were delays, often return visits, and invariably uncertainty. And once I was accepted to join a local doctor's surgery, a number of 'invitations' flooded in for this test and that, care of the National Health Service.

On an earlier visit to London, I had joined my local council's Walk for Health group and, whenever I could, I went walking through local parks, as much for an exchange of ideas and the sharing of knowledge as to improve my wellbeing and fitness. Despite this effort to stay on top of everything, I fell victim to pressure, an urge to get things done, and all this before I could even think about refurbishing my flat. By 6pm each evening I was exhausted. This meant I opened a bottle of wine and over the next couple of hours drank to the halfway mark. On a nightly basis, not a good idea.

I was also a serious imbiber of coffee. In the United States I drank decaf most of the time, particularly when I was working. I would write a few paragraphs then reward myself with coffee while contemplating the next few. Back in London, on my first morning, I grabbed a large tin of regular caffeinated coffee off a supermarket shelf, never anticipating any ill-effect. So, too much wine and too much caffeine. And one or other or both, plus the stress of moving, sent my blood pressure soaring.

My new NHS doctor (I was thrilled to finally meet her) was unhappy. I protested I had White Coat syndrome. She wanted to put me straight on medication but I begged to hold off until I'd bought a blood pressure monitor and tried taking a reading at home. I vaguely remembered the film "Something's Gotta Give" in which Jack Nicholson attempts to lower his blood pressure by closing his eyes and imagining he's by the sea in some exotic place with a loaded cocktail in hand. If I imagined the same sort of scenario, I was convinced all would be OK.

Very wisely, the doctor printed out advice sheets relating to causes and concerns of hypertension. Reading these at home, the possible correlation between blood pressure and caffeine became apparent. Alcohol too. The next morning I raced out and bought some decaf. And the following morning I cut my coffee intake to two cups of decaf at breakfast. By 4pm the same day, I had withdrawal symptoms. The ensuing headache packed a punch but the effect deterred me from alcohol. Over the next few days my blood pressure plummeted. Better still, I've kept up the routine. Nowadays I drink less caffeine and refrain from alcohol four days a week when I'm home alone.

My doctor called me a star. "Most people don't take much notice of what we say," she added sadly, which made me feel sorry for her. If I dished out professional advice in the knowledge much of it would go unheeded, I would be pretty depressed.

Part of my problem was undoubtedly linked to moving. Tense times affect everyone and, as I discovered, I wasn't quite in the clear. Yes, my mouth was rebelling. This time my new hygienist saw problems arising and alerted my new dentist who concurred I had a problem. Having thought I had one setback under control, there I was headed to a periodontist's surgery to confront another.

"I'm very conservative," he announced, attempting and failing to instil confidence. But, true to his word, he put me on a new and more vigorous cleaning regime involving lots of little picks, different colours, employed every night without fail. To me, anything seemed preferable to the scalpel. Not quite cured after two weeks, I did, however, return for a small spot of relatively minor gum surgery.

When you move from one country to another, finding products that you are used to can be difficult. Things look similar, even with identical packaging, but the effects can be devastatingly different. Take hair colour. I bought the same shade of hair colour manufactured by the same company in precisely the same wrapping as I had used in Florida. Nevertheless, this time instead of turning my greying hair a dazzling flaxen blonde, I emerged a redhead. This caused distress and more upset. I tried recolouring the same week (which you are advised not to do) but it still wasn't right. I wore a rain hat despite the sun because I didn't want anyone in the walking group to have a shock. Four colour changes later, I settled on another manufacturer and miraculously rediscovered the shade I used to be. I suppose it's all vanity but how one feels is important, don't you think?

I have to say the walking group was a godsend. A very pleasant help in trouble. Not about my hair but other queries. I would sound them out for all sorts of advice and was never disappointed. They knew of places to go, organisations to join, the right shops, and the cheapest way to get things done. A veritable source of information as well as friendship.

When I began refurbishing my flat, they were helpful about that too. I went to designated stores, pored through magazines and scoured the Internet. Looking at a picture and checking measurements first made shopping a breeze. I would pick and order during the day then unpack and install in the evenings. The one tedious part was dismantling the cardboard boxes after deliveries.

Today, now that it's done, I have time to reflect. I look in the mirror, consider the past and how much time lies ahead. Right now, thoughts of further travel are restricted by Covid but the world is opening up again, albeit slowly. Despite the anguish of environmentalists, airlines are reducing emissions and inventors are seeking less polluting ways to travel so, before I get too old, I have a few more trips to make and old friends to see. I don't have a bucket list, but if I had one wish it would be to ride as a passenger on the annual London to Brighton parade of old vehicles in November. Why I entertain such a thought is as much a mystery to me as anyone else, not least considering that I have managed to go through life never owning a car and not driving for the past forty years!

I have spent extended time in four countries – Britain, Australia, Armenia and USA, and shorter periods in many more. During the aftermath of World War II, I grew up in a country rebuilding and learning to have fun again. Rationing gave way to the hula hoop, perms to miniskirts, Vera Lynn to the Beatles. I toured the world, finding my feet for two years before returning to live in Sydney, Australia. A short interlude back in London in my 30s then it was off again, this time to New York with a new husband and a dear stepson. An earthquake in Armenia shook the upbeat status and it was on to Yerevan for two years before returning to the United States and apartment life in Florida. Finally, a return to London, back to the capital that most certainly will be my final home.

Reflection is no bad thing and for me life will always be about the people I met along the way. Those I have worked with, loved, or just met fleetingly like ships in the night. Past impressions return when prompted by something unforeseen, or stay forever. With them all, hovering, watchful and steadfast, has been my family. I began life with three sisters, Diana, Elizabeth and Mary. Of the three, the one yet to be mentioned is Diana, whose life took a different course to my own. A nursery nurse by profession, she married a welfare officer and together they became foster parents to more than sixty children, adopting one as well as having three of their own. My own voluntary work does not compare to her selfless and ongoing devotion.

We all live differently. Each to their own. But some of us have a much better chance to live their lives to the full than others, and here I count myself among the privileged. Despite the years, I look forward to sharing, giving and enjoying, which together make for contentment and return so much more in terms of fulfilment. The world will go on turning, peace will be an ongoing struggle with despots and tyrants forever seeking more land to rule and crushing those who stand in their way or raise a defiant hand. But the more pain they inflict, the more the rest of us are required to lead by example.